# Faith in Markets?

# FAITH IN MARKETS?

## Abrahamic Religions and Economics

EDITED BY BENEDIKT KOEHLER

with contributions from

DAVID CONWAY · BENEDIKT KOEHLER
ESA MANGELOJA · TOMI OVASKA
MARTIN RHONHEIMER · ALI SALMAN
NIMA SANANDAJI

Institute of
**Economic** Affairs

First published in Great Britain in 2023 by
The Institute of Economic Affairs
2 Lord North Street
Westminster
London SW1P 3LB
in association with London Publishing Partnership Ltd
www.londonpublishingpartnership.co.uk

The mission of the Institute of Economic Affairs is to improve understanding
of the fundamental institutions of a free society by analysing and expounding
the role of markets in solving economic and social problems.

A CIP catalogue record for this book is available from the British Library.

ISBN 978-0-255-36824-7

Many IEA publications are translated into languages other
than English or are reprinted. Permission to translate or to reprint
should be sought from the Director General at the address above.

Typeset in Kepler by T&T Productions Ltd
www.tandtproductions.com

Printed and bound by Hobbs the Printers Ltd

www.carbonbalancedprint.com
CBP2250

## CONTENTS

*About the authors*                                                        ix
*Foreword*                                                                 xiii
*Acknowledgements*                                                         xv
*List of tables and figures*                                              xvi

**1  Introduction: religion and economics                                  1**
*Benedikt Koehler*

The Enlightenment and after                                                2
Religion and economics                                                     5
This book                                                                  7

**2  The Middle East needs to rediscover its
    market roots                                                          11**
*Nima Sanandaji*

The first enterprises evolved in Babylonia and Assyria                    11
The invisible hand of the market in ancient Persia                        13
China and India independently created their own
    free-market traditions                                                18
The Middle Eastern industrial revolution                                  20
Ideological support for economic freedom began in
    the East                                                              21
A renaissance for markets in the East                                     28

**3 The economics of the books of Moses**     **30**
*Benedikt Koehler*

Moses: man or myth?     31
Israelite economics before Moses     32
Mosaic economics     36
The absence of theology from contemporaneous
    economics     42
Abrahamic economics versus Greek economics     44
The medieval and modern afterlife of Mosaic
    economics     46
Conclusion     53

**4 Muhammad's conception of property as a
bundle of rights**     **55**
*Benedikt Koehler*

The *waqf*     55
Introduction of *waqfs* by Muhammad     59
Reliability of sources     63
The evolution of trusts and corporations in
    Christendom     65
Implications for policy today     67
Summary     69

**5 The economics of property rights in early
and medieval Christianity**     **71**
*Benedikt Koehler*

Public munificence in Roman antiquity     72
Christian welfare in Carthage, Milan and
    Constantinople     75
Christian versus pagan welfare policies     85
Patristic economics in the literature     86
Medieval Christian discourse on property rights     90
Summary     97

6   **Sir Thomas More's *Utopia*: an overlooked economic classic**   **100**
*Esa Mangeloja and Tomi Ovaska*

The theological core of Utopia: common property   104
Economic concepts in *Utopia*   111
The fundamental goal of all economic systems   117
Defining and enforcing the rules of economic
  systems   119
Even if an economic system works, does it fulfil
  people's needs?   128
Conclusion   130
Appendix: The Hutterites   132

7   **Judaism and liberalism: Israel's economic problem with its Haredim**   **133**
*David Conway*

Judaism and liberalism   133
The principal varieties of contemporary liberalism   138
Why it is with classical liberalism that Judaism is in
  closest accord   141
Welfare provision as mandated in the Hebrew Bible   143
Welfare provision as mandated in rabbinic Judaism   146
The present-day relevance of Judaism's affinity with
  classical liberalism   152

8   **The true meaning of 'social justice': a Catholic view of Hayek**   **162**
*Martin Rhonheimer*

The problem of social justice talk   162
Hayek's criticism of social justice   164
The limits of Hayek's critique of social justice and
  the widening of the perspective   168

The social justice of capitalism and of the free
   market economy     178
Social justice in Catholic social doctrine     188
Conclusion     196

**9   The libertarian character of the Islamic
economy     199**
*Ali Salman*

Glossary of Islamic terms     199
The principles of economics in Islam     201
Islamic economics: signposts to statism     209
Conclusion     217

**References**     223

**About the IEA**     240

## ABOUT THE AUTHORS

## David Conway

David Conway is Emeritus Professor of Philosophy at Middlesex University, where he taught for over thirty years and was Head of its School of Philosophy and Religious Studies. He has also taught at the Universities of Essex, Roehampton and Malawi. After leaving Middlesex, he worked for a decade at the Westminster-based social policy research institute, Civitas. His publications include *A Farewell to Marx, Classical Liberalism, Free-Market Feminism, The Rediscovery of Wisdom, A Nation of Immigrants? A Brief Demographic History of Britain, Liberal Education and the National Curriculum* and *With Friends Like These: Why Britain Should Leave the European Union and How?*

## Benedikt Koehler

A Fellow in the Economics of Religion at the Institute of Economic Affairs, Dr Koehler studies the impact of Abrahamic religions on medieval economics and business. He has written biographies of Adam Müller (1980) and Ludwig Bamberger (1999) and is the author of *Early Islam and the Birth of Capitalism* (2014). He has also published on nineteenth-century intellectual and business history. He was educated at Yale, Tübingen and City University London.

## Esa Mangeloja

Currently working as a Senior Lecturer of Economics (University of Jyväskylä) and Adjunct Professor (Docent) of Economics (University of Tampere), Esa Mangeloja received a doctoral degree in 2001 with a dissertation on Nordic Stock Market Integration. In addition to his academic career, Dr Mangeloja worked for several years as a stock market analyst and financial strategist. His main research interests are in applied macroeconomics, particularly in questions related to economics of religion and economics of sport, in addition to themes of economic growth, finance and economic history. His research has been published in international journals and books.

## Tomi Ovaska

Having studied political science at the University of Jyväskylä in his native Finland, Tomi Ovaska moved to the US to pursue economics at graduate level. He took an MA and a PhD at West Virginia University and is now Distinguished Professor of Economics at Youngstown State University, Ohio. His research interests include behavioural economics, comparative economic systems and entrepreneurship. He is also Docent in political economy at his alma mater, the University of Jyväskylä.

## Martin Rhonheimer

Swiss-born Martin Rhonheimer studied history, philosophy, political science and theology in Zurich and Rome. He holds a Doctorate in Philosophy from the University of Zurich. In 1983 he was ordained a Catholic priest. From 1990 to 2020 he was Professor of Ethics and Political Philosophy at the Faculty of Philosophy of the Pontifical University of the Holy Cross in Rome. He remains associated with the university as a visiting professor. In 2014 he co-founded in Vienna (where he currently lives) the Austrian Institute of Economics and Social Philosophy (www.austrian-institute .org) of which he is the president. Father Rhonheimer is the author of many books and articles in the field of ethics, action theory and political philosophy.

## Ali Salman

Ali Salman is co-founder and CEO of Islam and Liberty Network, a global platform for researchers and academics active in Muslim-majority countries advancing understanding of religious, political and economic freedoms. He is the author of *Islam and Economics: Markets, Morality and Justice* (Acton, 2021) and several monographs and edited volumes. An economist by training, Ali Salman is also the founder and Executive Director of Policy Research Institute of Market Economy (PRIME), an independent economic policy think tank in Islamabad.

## Nima Sanandaji

Dr Nima Sanandaji is the director of the European Centre of Entrepreneurship and Policy Reform, and an entrepreneur. He has published in areas as diverse as economics, social sciences, history, biotechnology, polymer technology and physical chemistry. The author of thirty books, on topics such as policy reform, innovation, entrepreneurship, women's career opportunities, crime prevention and preventive social work, his favourite topic is the historical origins of the modern capitalist economy.

# FOREWORD

At the Institute of Economic Affairs we aim to conduct and promote research in economic and political matters and disseminate the results to improve public understanding of the institutions of a free society. Freedom of religion and of market exchange are clearly two important freedoms. But when they are linked, organised religion seems often to be treated as if it is some kind of antidote to the market. Many people seem to think that whatever merits a broadly market system may have, social justice must be supplied from somewhere else. And since religion – so it is presumed – is very much concerned with social justice, it must be seen in opposition to the market.

The essays in this book present one kind of challenge to this view. Looking into the origins and histories of the three major Abrahamic religions – Judaism, Christianity and Islam – the authors find market exchange to have been important in them all. So, to take one case, volume editor Benedikt Koehler argues in one of his contributions that property rights were essential in early Christianity. Koehler notes that early Christianity specifically linked property rights and poor relief in ways quite distinct from any attitude of the prior Roman world. In particular, in the work of Ambrose of Milan, private property offered the means of redemption through the provision of poor relief.

Furthermore, Koehler charts how the medieval controversy over Christ's ownership of property was ultimately resolved in favour of such ownership by Pope John XXII in 1329.

That is a sketch of one example of the kind of analysis offered in this collection. But the wider approach also deserves note. That is the approach of fully recognising the importance of the study of economic thought in a broad intellectual (and, in this case, religious) context. Adam Smith and his predecessors understood that intimately; it was the natural, probably unconscious aspect of the essence of their study. It has been far too often neglected in later work. This book offers a specific example of the kind of enquiry that should have so much more standing in our intellectual history.

The essays selected for the volume are reprinted from *Economic Affairs*, the refereed academic journal jointly produced by the IEA and the University of Buckingham, with acknowledgement to Wiley, the publisher. As always, the opinions expressed in this publication are those of the authors, and not of the IEA, which has no corporate view on any matters, whether economic, political or spiritual.

JAMES FORDER
*Research Director, Institute of Economic Affairs*
January 2023

## ACKNOWLEDGEMENTS

Chapters 2–9 originally appeared in *Economic Affairs*, the journal published by Wiley on behalf of the Institute of Economic Affairs and the University of Buckingham: chapter 2 (38(3), October 2018, pp. 348–56); chapter 3 (39(2), June 2019, pp. 251–63); chapter 4 (35(1), February 2015, pp. 52–59); chapter 5 (37(1), February 2017, pp. 112–24); chapter 6 (39(1), February 2019, pp. 65–80); chapter 7 (37(2), June 2017, pp. 240–53; chapter 8 (35(1), February 2015, pp. 35–51); chapter 9 (33(1), February 2013, pp. 108–18).

All chapters © Institute of Economic Affairs. Permissions for reuse can be obtained by using the RightsLink 'Request Permissions' link on Wiley Online Library.

## TABLES AND FIGURES

| Table 1 | Types of rule and means of enforcement | 121 |
| Table 2 | Attributes of economic systems | 123 |

| Figure 1 | Utopia in a systems map | 126 |
| Figure 2 | Maslow's hierarchy of needs | 129 |

# 1 INTRODUCTION: RELIGION AND ECONOMICS

Benedikt Koehler

Many religions have fostered market economics. However, Abrahamic faiths – those in which the figure of Abraham plays an important role – provide for economists of religion a particularly fertile field of study for economists of religion. This book gathers together a selection of articles that have appeared in the journal *Economic Affairs*. Its shared theme is to point out individual stages on the path to market economics taken in the three key faiths: Judaism, Christianity and Islam.[1]

Adherents of Abrahamic faiths have long insisted on drawing boundaries between each other, but in fact they have more in common than separates them. Seen against the relief of religions around the world, Abrahamic faiths form a distinct cultural unit. No other cluster of religions spread over a larger area and for a longer period.

Abrahamic religions exhibit innumerable examples of influences that travelled back and forth across denominational borders, and indeed the capacity to absorb external

---

1 There are other Abrahamic faiths, ranging from the Baha'i Faith to Rastafarianism, but these are the ones with the largest number of believers and the greatest influence.

influences has been a hallmark of Abrahamic faiths. One example is the very conception of Abrahamic faiths as religions. The term derives from an extra-Abrahamic source: *religio* was a borrowing from pagan Romans. An early researcher into the etymology of the term *religio*, St Augustine, derived it from the verb *ligare*, 'to bind', a verb that branches into connotations including *lex* (law) and *obligatio* (duty). The connotations of Latin *religio* included 'conscientiousness, sense of right, moral obligation, and duty' (translation from Lewis and Short (1879)). Another pagan Roman term whose connotations have similarly atrophied is *pietas*. Today it would be considered incongruous to apply the term 'pious' to someone who is an atheist. For Romans, by contrast, the meanings conveyed by *pietas* were 'dutiful conduct, sense of duty, devotion, affection for a parent' (ibid.). Although Christianity superseded Roman paganism, the pagan understanding of the connotations of religion obtained in Christianity until the waning of the Middle Ages: religion was a mental disposition governing everyday conduct.

## The Enlightenment and after

Religion began to lose its grip on culture and society with the advent of the Enlightenment. Once René Descartes, John Locke and Immanuel Kant had equipped philosophy to dispense with theology, religion was extruded from any field of enquiry other than theology. The status of religion as an authoritative frame of reference for scholarly discourse eroded further with the emergence of a new scholarly discipline in the nineteenth century, sociology. Two pioneers of sociology, August Comte and Karl Marx, dealt near-fatal blows against the study of religion in its own right.

August Comte posited a stadial evolution of human rationality: its three stages consisted of a theological, metaphysical and finally a positivist stage. But Comte felt that while traditional religion was obsolete, a new one needed to replace it, and he devised a new creed, positivism, replete with its own temples.

Karl Marx went further than Auguste Comte, aiming to dismantle religion altogether. Indeed, Marx acknowledged that there existed a causal link between religion, culture and the economy. But, as he posited, the direction of causation ran in the opposite direction to what had been thought. For Marx, religion was but the visible drapery hiding an economic backdrop. Yet Comte and Marx, notwithstanding their influence on the study of religion as a social phenomenon, were not to have the last word. The next generation of sociologists re-evaluated the ramifications of religion for social structure and its study revived. The turning point was marked by William Robertson Smith, a former Scottish seminarian, whose works, in particular *The Religion of the Semites* (1889), broke new ground in elucidating the interdependence between religious beliefs, kinship and institutions. His work came into the hands of Émile Durkheim, the first incumbent of a professorship of sociology in France, and put him in a position to oppose the Marxian assertion that religion was determined by economics. Against Marx, Durkheim countered that religion was the primal determinant of social conceptions. As he wrote in *Les Formes élémentaires de la vie religieuse* (Durkheim 1995: 421), '[a]ll the great social institutions were born in religion,' adding that, '[o]nly one form of social activity has not as yet been explicitly linked to religion: economic activity.'

Among Durkheim's many followers, one of the most notable was Max Weber, whose study of religion and of capitalism culminated in *The Protestant Ethic and the Spirit of Capitalism* (1905 [1930]). Weber linked the birth of capitalism (the term was introduced into sociology by Weber) to religion, and in this way opened a new field of sociological investigation. His approach was applied by R. H. Tawney (1926) to Protestantism, by Amintore Fanfani (1934) to Catholicism, and by Maxime Rodinson (1966) to Islam.

Meanwhile a new thread of enquiry into the social dimensions of religions was taken up by political philosophy. A thesis gained ground whereby the secularisation of political philosophy in the Enlightenment was illusory. On close inspection, political philosophy was a species of reconstituted theology, a secular shell of a theological core. Proponents of this assertion can be found across the spectrum of political outlooks, from rightists such as Carl Schmitt, to conservatives such as Leo Strauss and to libertarians such as John Rawls.[2] This theory has found support

---

2   Eric Nelson (2019) treated Rawls's engagement with the fourth-century Patristic theologian Pelagius in his *The Theology of Liberalism*.

also among philosophers in the US (Gillespie 2008) and in Europe (Agamben 1998).

## Religion and economics

In economics, engagement with the ramifications of religion progressed on a trajectory that differed from that in sociology and political science for a long time. Only in recent decades have these trajectories been converging.

Adam Smith was one of the pioneers focusing attention on the workings of economic incentives in religious institutions. In *The Wealth of Nations*, a section 'On the expense of the institutions for the instruction of people of all ages' pointed out that a clergy funded by voluntary contributions would be more responsive to the needs of their congregation than one funded by tax.[3] Smith also anticipated the secularisation theory, the predicate of which states that affiliation to religion weakens once societies grow richer and better educated.[4]

Adam Smith's pointer was ahead of its time – economists did not elaborate the secularisation theory until the

---

3   Smith (1776 [1937]: 740): '[The clergy] may either depend altogether for their subsistence upon the voluntary contributions of their hearers; or they may derive it from some other fund to which the law of their country may entitle them; such as a landed estate, a tythe or land tax, an established salary or stipend. Their exertion, their zeal and industry, are likely to be much greater in the former situation than in the latter' (*The Wealth of Nations*, Book 5, Part 3, Article 3).

4   'The gradual improvements of arts, manufactures, and commerce, the same causes which destroyed the power of the great barons, destroyed in the same manner, through the greater part of Europe, the whole temporal power of the clergy.' (ibid. p. 755)

twentieth century. In the nineteenth century, when economics emerged as an academic discipline in the US, many early American academicians gravitated to the field following prior training in theology. Francis Wayland, author of *The Elements of Political Economy* (1837), was a Baptist minister. John Bates Clark, a president of the American Economic Association, was in his early career a proponent of Christian Socialism. Henry Ward Beecher, a prominent theologian of America's Gilded Age, preached the Prosperity Gospel, extolling his Park Avenue congregation to strive for riches as a sign of God's blessing.

Meanwhile the marginalist school of economics was incurious about the economics of religion. Economics-led research into religion began, however, to gain pace in recent decades, and has branched out into diverse avenues of enquiry. Notable achievements included Timur Kuran's *The Long Divergence: How Islamic Law Held Back the Middle East* (2010), which exposed religious origins of institutional stasis in Islamic societies; Larry Siedentop's *Inventing the Individual: The Origins of Western Liberalism* (2014), which rooted the dynamism of Western economic entrepreneurship in medieval Christianity; and Joseph Henrich's *The Weirdest People in the World: How the West became Psychologically Peculiar and Particularly Prosperous* (2020), which ascribed attitudes to risk-taking and trust in social institutions to social conditioning by early Christian kinship practices. More examples could be added – interdisciplinary collaboration between economists and neighbouring disciplines is not any longer uncommon.

Two literature reviews of the economics of religion published nearly twenty years apart in the *Journal of Economic Literature* (Iannaccone 1998; Iyer 2016) document its progress. If the 1998 review pointed out that the economics of religion still lacked a JEL code, the 2016 review could report that that omission had been corrected.[5] The introduction of a discrete JEL code showed that the economics of religion in the meantime had established itself as a growing field of economic research. Robert Barro and Rachel McCleary have recently provided an overview of the many branches of economics of religion in *The Wealth of Religions* (2019).

## This book

Adam Smith, Émile Durkheim and F. A. Hayek were conscious that culture and economics exhibit multifarious interactions. The economics of religion has assimilated the understanding of religion as it prevailed in antiquity, namely economic investigation into behaviours relating to 'conscientiousness, sense of right, moral obligation, and duty.' The shared intent of the contributions to this book is to illustrate how behaviours and attitudes guided by *religio* permeated the three Abrahamic faiths, and inclined their adherents towards behaviours that tended to market economics. From earliest Mesopotamian history, market economics had a protean capacity to advance in

---

5   *Journal of Economic Literature* (JEL) alphanumeric codes classify publications by subject matter.

diverse contexts of cultures and creeds, and theological boundaries delimiting Abrahamic faiths did not impede the crossover of economic best practices from one religion to another. The Mosaic conception of the right to own land was dominant in medieval Christianity; the Mosaic ban on usury persists to this day in Islam; and the Islamic legal frame of a charitable entity, the *waqf*, was a template for the Common Law trust in England.

In the modern secular world, religion and economics no longer share the same frame of reference. Our book contributes a liberal perspective to the dialogue between religious faiths and secular markets.

In the next chapter Nima Sanandaji gives an overview of incipient market economics in Mesopotamia before the advent of Abrahamic religions. The following three chapters review the proximate ramifications of the teaching of Moses, Jesus and Muhammad for economic practices.

In the first of these, Benedikt Koehler argues that Moses was a foundational figure in the history of economic thought. Moses brought the regulation of property rights, welfare and trade into the realm of religion, and thereby removed it from control by secular authorities. In the next chapter Koehler shows that Muhammad emulated Moses by invoking the authority of his prophetic office to frame the dispositions of property ownership and of welfare provision. Muhammad overturned Mesopotamian welfare practices through crafting a legal distinction between rights to own and rights to use property. Koehler then goes on in chapter 4 to show that early Christians followed the Mosaic precept whereby the right to own property entailed a duty to provide welfare. Christians debated throughout the Middle Ages how a duty to provide welfare could be reconciled with the right to own property. Notably Francis of Assisi held that Christianity altogether rejected ownership of property; Thomas Aquinas rebutted this assertion. On the eve of the Reformation Pope John XXII declared that Christian doctrine approved of the right to private property.

After the Middle Ages, the monopoly of religion as a frame of reference for economic dispositions had come to an end. In their chapter Esa Mangeloja and Tomi Ovaska focus on Sir Thomas More's *Utopia* (1516), a book that was representative of a new, post-medieval approach to economics. By imagining an economic system based on philosophical principles rather than on theological tenets, Thomas More instigated a new genre of 'utopian' political and economic literature.

The final three chapters focus on the frictions that the social thought of Judaism, Christianity and Islam encounter in their respective contemporary secular settings. In his essay, David Conway contrasts the reception of Moses in the secular West with that in Israel. Moses is invoked by secular legislators in the West to advocate classical liberalism, but is used by devout Haredim in Israel to claim support for statist welfare practices. In his contribution on the true meaning of 'social justice', Martin Rhonheimer aims to reconcile the notions of justice in Catholic social teaching with F. A. Hayek's ideas. Finally, Ali Salman exposes the contradictions between influential Islamic economists inclined towards state-directed welfare policies and price controls, and *shari'a* guidance that endorses competition and bans price control.

The essays in this book provide an insight into a rich and growing literature on Abrahamic faiths and their teaching on the role of markets, a literature which is not simply a scholarly diversion but which has deep implications for the conduct of believers and the societies they inhabit.

# 2 THE MIDDLE EAST NEEDS TO REDISCOVER ITS MARKET ROOTS

Nima Sanandaji

## The first enterprises evolved in Babylonia and Assyria

Today, cities such as New York, London, Stockholm, Singapore and Hong Kong are known for their commerce, enterprise and vibrant urban life. Middle Eastern cities such as Mosul and Aleppo are, in contrast, scenes of devastation. Yet for much of human history Mosul and Aleppo were important centres of the global market network, which facilitated the exchange of valuable goods, the flow of ideas, and migration. Free markets have deep roots in the history of the Middle East. Mosul and Aleppo are just two of many examples of the enterprising history of the region.

It is widely believed that free markets, individual liberty and limited government are modern concepts with roots in Western society. However, in fact these ideals and institutions have a much older Eastern origin. The first market economies of the world developed in present-day Iraq and Syria, the countries in which Mosul and Aleppo respectively are located. It was here that the first entrepreneurs, the first enterprises, the first banks and the first financial speculators emerged around 4,000 years ago.

Over time, a large number of clay tablets from these civilisations have been found and deciphered. Many of these tablets are records of economic transactions, and they paint a clear picture: Middle Eastern civilisations prospered and fostered human progress because they were largely market-driven. Surviving accounts even tell us how the market prices in ancient Babylon fluctuated from month to month. As Dutch historians Robartus Johannes van der Spek and Kees Mandemakers (2003: 533) conclude, 'That market mechanisms played their part in the Babylonian economy seems now to be unquestionable'.

The defining characteristic of a market economy is that factor markets play a dominant role in the allocation of capital and other factors of production. Market economies require a high degree of monetisation, which means that trade is based on currency rather than exchange of one good for another. Michael Jursa (2015: 103) explains that Babylonia achieved a far-reaching monetisation of economic exchange which went hand in hand with urbanisation, demographic expansion and increased productivity per capita. The result was 'a dynamic economic system that was strongly market-oriented', although households continued to retain some level of self-sufficiency.

Around one millennium later, the ancient Western civilisations of Greece and Rome imported the concept of enterprise from the Middle East. But the ancient Greeks and Romans never embraced it wholeheartedly. Whereas the ancient Middle Easterners viewed commerce and enterprise in a positive light, the Greeks and Romans regarded them as low-status work, which should be left to foreigners, freedmen of low standing, and slaves. Consequently, the business leaders, merchant ship captains and bank managers of ancient Greece and Rome were often natives of the Middle East.

## The invisible hand of the market in ancient Persia

This market tradition persisted in the Persian Empire, founded by Cyrus the Great, which in 480 BC is estimated to have accounted for 44 per cent of the global population, a historic record.[1] The Greek mercenary general and historian Xenophon is famed, through his writings, for having inspired Alexander the Great to invade Persia. He also wrote about the economic practices in the Persian Empire, perhaps to inspire his fellow Greeks to abandon their distrust of the market economy.

Today it is widely assumed that it was Adam Smith, the father of modern economics, who first described the phenomenon of specialisation in the marketplace. Accompanying this view is the idea that the first well-functioning market economies developed in Europe, and that Adam Smith was the first to describe how the invisible hand of the market made society prosperous. Yet, in fact, Xenophon gave an almost identical description of specialisation in the marketplace when writing about the economy of

---

1   http://www.guinnessworldrecords.com/world-records/largest-empire
    -by-percentage-of-world-population/

ancient Persia, 2,000 years before Adam Smith was born. Alexander Grey (1933: 32) provides a modern translation of Xenophon's *Cyropaedia* (*c.* 370 BC):

> For in small towns the same workman makes chairs and doors and ploughs and tables, and often this same artisan builds houses, and even so he is thankful if he can only find employment to support him. And it is, of course, impossible for a man of many trades to be proficient in all of them. In large cities, on the other hand, inasmuch as many people have demands upon each branch of industry, one trade alone, and very often even less than a whole trade, is enough to support a man: one man, for instance, makes shoes for men, and another for women; and there are places even where one man earns a living by only stitching shoes, another by cutting them out, another by sewing the uppers together, while there is another who performs none of these operations but only assembles the parts. It follows, therefore, as a matter of course, that he who devotes himself to a very specialized line of work is bound to do it in the best possible manner.

The invisible hand of the market was evidently already at work in the Middle East in the fourth century BC.

## The first account of free-market policy

Additionally, Xenophon's retelling of a Persian story includes the world's first known defence of voluntary market exchange. Xenophon's story concerned Cyrus the Great, arguably the most important political figure of his time. The story is about the education of young Cyrus, who was given legal cases to adjudicate by his teachers in order to prepare him for a future as a law-abiding king (Gera 1993: 74):

> Cyrus tells Mandane that he was quite successful as a judge, but was once punished for producing an ill-judged verdict. The Persian prince's case here is a provocative one, and Xenophon adroitly makes use of it to turn from the Persian interest in justice to very Greek controversies on the topic. When a tall boy forcibly exchanges his too small coat for a smaller boy's too large one, Cyrus decides that each boy should keep the better-fitting coat. His teachers then flogged him for the verdict, explaining that it was his task to judge, not the fit of the garment, but its rightful owner. The coat had been taken by force, and since what is lawful is just and what is unlawful is violent or unjust, Cyrus must decide a case according to the law.

The moral of this story is that a wise ruler should not regulate the marketplace based on what the ruler believed to be an efficient exchange. Rather, he should only concern himself with whether the transaction had been conducted in accordance with property rights and voluntary exchange. That is the essence of free enterprise. And the story is the earliest known detailed account of free-market economic policy.

## *Zoroastrianism and Islam support free enterprise*

The ancient Persian faith of Zoroastrianism has an interesting connection with markets. The core of this religion is
the teachings of the prophet Zoroaster, who in his Gathas
– a collection of 17 hymns written some 3,700 years ago –
formulated strong arguments for investing resources in
the first permanent settlements and for trade between
them, rather than in the impulsively destructive and
short-sighted surrounding nomadic tribes. Zoroastrianism here differs radically from Christianity and Judaism in
that this philosophical tradition is supportive of material
wealth accumulation and self-reliance. Zoroastrianism
also harbours the first defence of egalitarianism known in
the history of ideas. It is consequently a religion defending both equality between the sexes and the recycling of
limited resources while opposing slavery. It is no coincidence that Cyrus the Great is cited in the Bible for having
freed the Jewish people from slavery and allowed them to
return to their ancestral lands. The Zoroastrian tradition
was pro-market and anti-slavery, quite the opposite of the
tradition of the ancient Greeks and Romans.

According to the Zoroastrian faith, justice is objective,
and the law – which is based on justice – is an objective
precept that even the king must follow. An important element in the development of the Western market economic
model is the gradual shift from tyranny towards the rule
of law, specifically respecting the property rights of the
common citizen. The Persians likewise believed that even
a great king would stray from the right path if he failed to

recognise the importance of private property rights. Zoro-astrianism is no longer a widely followed religion but is confined to a small community living mostly in Iran and India. The Indian Zoroastrians, called the Parsi, are few in number yet play a key role in the Indian business world. They run several of the largest business conglomerates in India. One example is the Tata family, which through the Tata Group manages a wide array of businesses in steel, car manufacturing, consultancy, energy, teleservices, and beverages, and owns the European car brands Jaguar and Land Rover. The Godrej and Wadia families, likewise of Parsi origin, own similar business conglomerates. The Zoroastrian faith's sanctioning of wealth accumulation, as well as its strong injunctions against lying, encourage its followers to become, and succeed as, entrepreneurs.

Islam, which became the dominant religion of the re-gion following Zoroastrianism, also evolved in a market-friendly environment, and largely supports free enterprise. Before the rise of Islam even the deep deserts of the Ara-bian Peninsula hosted cities that thrived on the specialised manufacture and export of goods such as perfumes. The Arab tradition of trade lives on in the faith and traditions of Islam. The Prophet Muhammed himself was a merchant for many years. He married his first wife, Khadija, a re-nowned merchant capitalist, after having managed some of her trade affairs. Khadija is seen as one of the most im-portant female figures in Islam, and is commonly regarded by Muslims as the 'Mother of the Believers'. She is a rare example of a female entrepreneur in the Middle Ages who has made an impact on history. When the Quraysh tribe in

Mecca gathered its caravans to embark upon the summer journey to Syria or the winter journey to Yemen, Khadija's caravan equalled in size the caravans of all other traders of the tribe put together (Ibn Sa'd 1995: 10).

## China and India independently created their own free-market traditions

The Middle East is not the only place where the practices and intellectual tradition of free markets emerged. Enterprise, banking and market-based exchange evolved independently later in China and India. A rich intellectual tradition in defence of economic liberty and against state involvement in the economy also emerged. The Chinese thinker Mencius, born around 2,400 years ago, is besides Confucius himself, the second most influential Confucian philosopher. Mencius argued in favour of protecting private property, emphasised the importance of market competition, opposed monopolies and explained that individuals constitute the fundamentals of the country. Laozi, the founder of Taoism, was perhaps the first libertarian thinker. He believed that government with its 'laws and regulations more numerous than the hairs of an ox' was an oppressor of the individual, and should be feared more 'than fierce tigers' (Rothbard 2006: 23).

The *Guanzi*, an important political text from ancient China (*c.*700 BC), contains a description of the invisible hand of the free marketplace. The 'Tale of the moneyed rat trader' is an old Indian folk tale which explains how voluntary market exchange and capital accumulation can allow even the most impoverished individual to climb the social ladder. Popular tales of the Middle East are also supportive of free enterprise. For a long time, Baghdad was one of the wealthiest cities in the world, as seen in the stories of the *One Thousand and One Nights* collection of Middle Eastern folk tales. In these tales, the heroes are often merchant capitalists, who – through their pursuit of wealth – benefit themselves as well as the rest of society. The Eastern tradition of portraying entrepreneurs as heroes differs sharply from the modern Western tradition, in which the agent of an economic enterprise is often the villain, while the hero is characterised by a disregard for material wealth. Modern Western institutions are shaped in accordance with the principles of the market economy, but contemporary Western culture still retains a hostile view of enterprise, commerce and wealth accumulation. In contrast, these things are all celebrated in Middle Eastern cultures.

Of course, the market-based exchange was not the only economic model in place in the historic Middle East, China and India; it competed with feudalism, tribalism and state control. In rural areas, much of the population consisted mostly of self-sufficient farmers. Yet in several cities in the Middle East, North Africa, India and China, mature and durable market institutions had emerged. The Silk Road bound together these market centres, and merchants brought the goods from Middle Eastern market cities such as Aleppo to Europe and Africa. Today, the story of globalisation and commerce is told almost exclusively from a Western viewpoint. However, much of the development occurred in the East and the South. Zanzibar and other trading cities across the Swahili coast, for example, grew wealthy by attracting African, Arab, Persian, Malaysian, Indonesian, Indian and Chinese merchants.

## The Middle Eastern industrial revolution

The Eastern market tradition was not 'simply about trade', a common description in Western economic thinking used to marginalise the role of the East in economic development. During the Islamic golden age (from the eighth century to the fourteenth century), water mills and windmills were used to create early mechanical power, which produced mechanised labour. A miniature industrial revolution occurred around the eleventh century, in which Middle Eastern factory complexes turned out ceramics, astronomical instruments, mechanical hydro- and wind-powered machinery, perfumes and weapons. The knowledge generated in these industries was transmitted to Europe. For example, Egyptian craftsmen in Greece established early glass factories in Europe in the eleventh century (Syed et al. 2011: 55).

The Damascus swords forged in Syria and wielded by Middle Eastern armies during the Crusades were made of such advanced materials that Europeans never managed to reproduce them. Only recently have scientists been able to understand the secrets of the swords: somehow, the Middle Eastern steelmakers managed to incorporate carbon nanotubes in the steel structure. This feat is quite astonishing given that carbon nanotubes were originally believed to be a product of modern nanotechnology.

For thousands of years, the Middle East prospered through enterprise. Persian carpets and Turkish delight were some of the most sought-after consumer goods of the early modern age; these products are still well known around the world. Coffee shops are similarly an invention of the Islamic world, having much in common with the tea houses in which Middle Eastern traders for centuries gathered to rest and make deals. Cotton, silk, olives, phosphates and oil products are examples of other goods exported from the Middle East and North Africa to Europe during the Middle Ages and the early modern age.

## Ideological support for economic freedom began in the East

Ideas of economic freedom often evolved in the Middle East, North Africa, China and India long before they reached the West. An example of this is the Laffer curve. One afternoon in 1974, the American economist Arthur Laffer met with Donald Rumsfeld, then US President Gerald Ford's chief of staff, and Dick Cheney, Rumsfeld's deputy, and explained that the relationship between tax revenues and the tax rate was not as simple as one would expect. As government tax rates increase, the taxable economy diminishes in size, and so increasing the tax rate might even result in lower revenues. This was relevant information at a time when the highest marginal tax rate of the US was fully 70 per cent. Since then, the Laffer curve has been used by supporters of low taxes around the world to reinforce their ideas. In the US, it helped to inspire a downward shift in taxation. US

President Ronald Reagan introduced massive changes in the 1980s, which reduced the marginal income tax rate of the US to 28 per cent. Since then, taxes have again risen to a rate of around 40 per cent. However, even the proponents of high tax policy are aware of Laffer's warnings: there is a limit to how high taxes can be raised in order to increase revenue.

While Laffer's theory proved to be a powerful tool in changing tax policy, it was not a new discovery. Laffer was rediscovering an idea that had been acknowledged during the golden age of Islamic free-market policy. Laffer (2004: 3) has himself explained that he did not invent the curve:

> The Laffer Curve, by the way, was not invented by me. For example, Ibn Khaldun, a 14th century Muslim philosopher, wrote in his work *The Muqaddimah*: 'It should be known that at the beginning of the dynasty, taxation yields a large revenue from small assessments. At the end of the dynasty, taxation yields a small revenue from large assessments.'

Ibn Khaldun was one of the main Islamic golden age intellectuals, and explained the rise and fall of entire dynasties by reference to stifling levels of taxation.

Hamid S. Hosseini (2003) explains that medieval Muslim writers held a much more favourable view of economic activity and wealth accumulation than contemporary Christian thinkers. Hosseini cites several influential Persian Muslim thinkers who praised wealth accumulation and self-interest. He notes: 'In contrast to their European counterparts, medieval Muslim writers praised economic activity and the accumulation of wealth, viewed individuals as acquisitive, and scorned poverty' (2003: 36).

Numerous intellectual works from this period favour free markets, limited government and limited taxation. In *Qabus Nameh*, a major work of Persian literature from the eleventh century, the mythological king of Iran, Kai Kavus, advised his son on economic matters. The ideas of rational self-interest expressed in this work lie very close to the thinking of Western free-market intellectuals such as Adam Smith and Ayn Rand (Hosseini 2003: 36). Nasreddin Hodja, a satirical philosopher who followed the Islamic mystical tradition of Sufism and lived in present-day Turkey during the thirteenth century, is still remembered through his popular stories. One of his ideas was that wise rulers should reduce the burden of taxation, for otherwise their kingdoms would collapse like a broken wall (Hariyanto 1995: 23–24).

## *A true wonder of the world: underground channels made possible by capitalism*

If we remain unaware of the Eastern origins of the free-market model, this will impair our understanding of the power of voluntary exchange and property rights. For example, hospitals and the medical sciences were largely developed in Persia, Arabia, India and China, to a great degree as private businesses. Another example is the qanats, a hidden wonder of the world which were built by market forces. These underwater irrigation systems, which were first constructed in Iran some 3,000 years ago, are the reason why civilisation could prosper in dry countries such as Iran, Syria and parts of Europe. The qanats, sometimes built hundreds of metres underground and running for kilometres at an exact angle, are astonishing feats of human engineering. Thousands of these impressive structures were built to irrigate previously barren lands, and remained in use for millennia. As late as 1968, most of the water used in Iran still came from this ancient infrastructure (Wulff 1968).

The qanats were made possible by property rights: those who irrigated previously dry land acquired ownership of the land and the water supplied to it. Those who built them were specialist private contractors. The contrast with the pyramids of Egypt is complete: the pyramids were built as massive symbols of government power, funded by oppressive rulers, and served little, if any, real-world purpose. The construction of the qanats was based on voluntary principles, and made it possible for countless generations of people to thrive in otherwise barren lands.

## Western capitalism is a continuation of Eastern capitalism

In the early modern age, Western capitalism arose as a more sophisticated economic model than earlier forms of Eastern capitalism. The Western form of capitalism was born in Italian city states such as Florence, Venice and Genoa. Already at the beginning of the thirteenth century, these city states had begun developing sophisticated market institutions. The merchant class formed a strong political faction in these cities, and it pushed for protection of property rights and a system of relatively free enterprise. Private workshops in the cities produced clothes, shoes, glassware, leatherwork, jewellery, elaborate metalwork, and other goods to be sold in other cities and countries.

Why did modern capitalism take its first steps in the Italian city states? It should first be noted that these cities were autonomous and dependent on trade. The absence of centralised state control allowed the cities to experiment with economic policies, and the merchant class was in favour of a free market. Geographical factors meant that the cities had good prospects for growth through enterprise. Florence, for example, became one of Europe's greatest industrial cities. The entrepreneurs of the city took advantage of the fast-flowing Arno River, which provided access to the sea for trade, as well as water power for the wheels of industry. Over time, the merchants of Florence transformed the local wool industry into an international business: buying wool from places such as Britain and transforming it into fine cloth. While early banking had evolved already around 2,000 BC in ancient Babylonia and Assyria, advanced banking practices evolved in the Italian city states some 3,000 years later during the Renaissance. In particular, they developed in Florence, and spread from there to other parts of Italy, to the rest of Europe and later to the world.

The Italian market model was in many ways revolutionary. It was arguably a more sophisticated model of free enterprise than anything that had ever existed before. Yet it did not develop in a vacuum. Rather, Italian proto-capitalism built upon inspiration from the market economy that had existed in the Middle East and North Africa during the Islamic golden age – a market tradition with which the Italian entrepreneurs had considerable trade relationships. One illustration of the historical importance of the Italian market model is that it was the birthplace of modern accounting. Yet this practice seems also to have been a further development of practices in Islamic societies.

Accounting is an important part of a business venture. A simple economic activity, such as a local shoemaker producing shoes for the people in a small village, can be carried out without detailed bookkeeping. But when businesses and the market networks through which they operate become more sophisticated, bookkeeping becomes vital. Large-scale manufacturers, importers and exporters of shoes have to keep track of the stocks in different wares, the prices at which the leather for the shoes is bought, the labour cost, the transportation cost and the prices at which the shoes are sold. Accounting practices were developed in the Italian city states, yet imported from the Middle East. Some Italian merchants at the time even wrote their accounts in Arabic numerals (Nobes 2001).

### *The Jewish community linked Eastern and Western capitalism*

One Middle Eastern group in particular was an important driving force in the development that occurred in Spain as well as Italy and the rest of Europe: the Jews. It should not come as a surprise that the Jewish community has played a key part in the development of the market economy. People of Jewish origin have for centuries played a key role in the market practices of Europe as well as the Middle East, in their role as bankers and entrepreneurs. It is no coincidence that the anti-capitalist ideologies of National Socialism and Marxism have relied on negative caricatures of Jews as capitalists; they were envied for their commercial success.

The Jewish community often turned to trade and banking for a number of institutional and religious reasons. Local rulers and church officials in Europe often discriminated against the Jews by preventing them access to many occupations, on the grounds that the Jews were socially inferior. Yet the members of this community were allowed to operate as moneylenders as well as tax collectors. Moneylending was seen as a sin forbidden to Christians, but officials understood that the practice was nevertheless needed. In line with the anti-commercial sentiments that for long existed in Christian Europe, moneylending was regarded as a necessary evil to be left to Jews. Also, many among the Jewish community could read at a time when the vast majority of people were illiterate, since Jewish religious customs required individuals be able to read the holy scriptures. All of this meant that the Jews had good reason to assume the role of moneylenders in Europe. For similar reasons, it was often Jews who were moneylenders in the Middle East and North Africa.

## A renaissance for markets in the East

Understanding the Eastern roots of free markets and free market economic theory is not just an exercise in history, or a way to strengthen the case for economic freedom; it is also a vital tool for advancing the new frontiers of capitalism. The reason is simply that the East can return to its free-market roots. China in particular has over the last two and a half millennia seen its economic policies shift forward and back – from the laissez-faire model of free exchange to central government control. During the second half of the twentieth century a failed experiment with Marxism/Maoism led to tens of millions of Chinese starving to death. Market reforms that began in the 1980s saw China return to its capitalist roots. In 1990, more than 60 per cent of people in East Asia lived in extreme poverty – the people of China and its neighbours were in some instances poorer than those who lived in Africa. Now only 3.5 per cent of those who live in this region are extremely poor. This shows how a culture with a long tradition of enterprise can relatively quickly catch up in terms of prosperity. Currently, a similar transition from poverty to wealth is happening in India.

But what about the Middle East? The region has thrived for millennia through enterprise. It can again bloom through market exchange. The present era, when the Middle East is associated with sectarian violence, oil dependency and statist control, is after all more of a historical aberration than the normal state of the region. Iranians, Arabs, Turks, Kurds, Assyrians, Jews and the myriad other groups in the Middle East have much that sets them apart, but they are all natural dealers and hagglers. Throughout its history, the region has been ravaged by wars countless times. Some of these – such as the brutal invasions of the Mongols and Timur – left deep and lasting scars. Yet Middle Eastern societies have always bounced back, not by relying on the riches provided by oil but rather through commerce and enterprise. Why should the modern age, in which the market economy has become a global phenomenon, be the exception?

A market renaissance of the Middle East is a viable path for our time, especially when Marxist ideology and oil dependency are gradually losing their grip on the region. The Western world can certainly encourage such a transformation, by relying more on free exchange than foreign intervention in the form of 'nation building' and war. The part of the world which is today known for endless conflict might in a few decades again be known as the birthplace of capitalism. This is an admirable goal to strive for.

# 3 THE ECONOMICS OF THE BOOKS OF MOSES

Benedikt Koehler

Moses derived economics from theology. Since no theological dimension was present in the economics of pre-Mosaic Israel, of Egypt and Babylonia, and of Greece and Rome, the theological turn of Mosaic economics was an innovation in the history of economic thought. The literature on Moses' unique contribution to economics is scarce, and where disquisitions on the economics of Judaism touch on Moses at all they tend to consider Mosaic economics as an early stage of Judaic economics, superseded by stages that followed.

One reason for this relative neglect may be that studies of Judaic economics need to cover so wide a spectrum of topics that Mosaic economics may seem but one of a myriad of moments. The economics of Moses, however, merits individual attention: Moses mapped a path for economics as conceived in all three Abrahamic religions, and his conceptions of the right to own land were foundational for economic discourse from the era of the Pentateuch until the Western Enlightenment – from *c.* 1,300 BC until the eighteenth century, to wit, some three millennia. This article tracks the transition from pre-Mosaic to Mosaic economics.[1]

## Moses: man or myth?

The Five Books of Moses, also known as the Pentateuch, changed their narrative character from the first to the second half: Genesis and Exodus revolved around events and personalities; Leviticus, Numbers and Deuteronomy progressively shaded into exposition of customs, rituals and laws. Multiple authors redacted the Pentateuch, which has encouraged the presumption that Moses might have been a fictitious person, or, even if historical, a person on whom certain attributes were projected. This presumption has good grounds. The very name of Moses – in Egyptian, Moses means 'one who is born' – adds weight to the view that Moses stood for an Everyman whose life was a paradigm for the human condition. Further, even if one were to grant the historicity of Moses, it would be impossible to show whether Mosaic economics ever mattered in practice. But for the argumentation of this article, it has no bearing whether Mosaic pronouncements were made by him or put into his mouth, whether they were observed or

---

1   The elaboration of Mosaic economics in post-Mosaic Judaism is outside this chapter's scope. To be clear, Judaic economics is not coterminous with the study of the economics of Jews (say, the propensity of individual Jews to pursue particular professions) or the study of the economics of Jewry (say, the study of philanthropic activities of Jewish collectives). Judaic economics, in contradistinction, is concerned with economics derived from the Hebrew Bible. Obviously, borders between these three fields are porous.

ignored: what is paramount is that precepts established by Moses were held to be normative.

Moses had a very different upbringing from that of the patriarchs. Abraham, Isaac and Jacob had lived their lives in tents; Moses had grown up in a palace; they earned their living from shepherding; he turned Israelites from shepherding to farming. Even if the Bible conflated fact and fiction, it was remarkable how well the recitation of formative experiences in Moses' upbringing and education comported with his economics. According to the Bible, Moses was raised by an Egyptian princess; he fled to Midian, where his father-in-law inducted him to priestly duties; and he led the Israelites out of Egypt and through Sinai to Canaan. His economics reflected such experiences: having been raised by a princess with siblings raised by slaves would have bred in him an acute sense of social inequality; having been exposed to Egyptian and Babylonian commerce would have taught him to compare and choose between economic practices; and having been educated as a priest would have inclined him to assert theological sanction for his leadership. Mosaic economics matched this formation: Moses' social bias was egalitarian; he adapted Egyptian and Babylonian practices; and – the most significant of his innovations – he based economic prescriptions on the will of God.

## Israelite economics before Moses

The earliest Israelites strove to acquire wealth, but their wealth, such as it was, did not include land. They by and large were shepherds or farmers, sometimes both. Cain was a farmer and Abel a shepherd; Cain turned from farming to shepherding after his expulsion from the community. Abraham's wealth consisted exclusively of movable property. The Book of Genesis pointed out that Abraham was acquisitive, 'And Abram was very rich in cattle, in silver, and in gold' (Gen. 13. 2). Land, on the other hand, was conspicuous by its absence in a detailed inventory of his estate listed by one of his slaves: 'The Lord has greatly blessed my master, and he has become rich: he has given him sheep and cattle, silver and gold, male and female slaves, camels and asses' (Gen. 24: 35). Only once did Abraham purchase land, for a burial plot for his wife Sara. His bid was not motivated by investment considerations; as Abraham pleaded: 'I am a stranger and a sojourner with you: give me a possession of a burying a place with you, that I may bury my dead out of my sight' (Gen. 23. 4).

Jacob likewise bought a parcel of land only once; and as with Abraham, his bid was from considerations of piety rather than of commerce (Gen. 33. 18–20):

> And Jacob came to Shalem, a city of Shechem, which is in the land of Canaan, when he came from Padan-aram; and pitched his tent before the city. And he bought a parcel of field, where he had spread his tent, at the hand of the children of Hamor, Shechem's father, for an hundred pieces of money. And he erected there an altar, and called it El-elohe-Israel.

As Israelites were landless, they relied on the goodwill of landed neighbours to let them graze their herds. Nomadic shepherds on the whole were denied the right to buy land, and Israelites were conscious that such entailed that their legal status was precarious. Indeed, Cain after his expulsion from his community lamented: 'I shall be a fugitive and a vagabond in the earth; and it shall come to pass, that every one that findeth me shall slay me' (Gen. 5: 14). Israelites were kept at a distance from their hosts. Thus, when the people of Shechem sold Jacob a plot of land they insisted such did not entitle him to free access to the town ('he camped before the town' (Gen. 33: 18–19)). Only when later they felt they needed to appease him – for reasons outside our scope here – did they hold out the prospect of further purchases of land and made a point of advertising this would raise his legal standing: 'You will dwell among us and the land will be open before you; settle, move about, and acquire holdings in it' (Gen. 34: 10). Shepherds also had low social status. When Israelites came to settle in Egypt, their brother Joseph cautioned them to introduce themselves as 'handlers of livestock' (Gen. 46: 32) and impressed on them to be under no illusion where they stood in the social order: 'That ye shall say, Thy servants' trade hath been about cattle from our youth even unto now, both we, his and also our fathers: that ye may dwell in the land of Goshen; for every shepherd is an abomination unto the Egyptians' (Gen. 46: 34).

Given that the patriarchs strove to accumulate wealth, it seems odd that they were indifferent to acquiring title to land, content to roam on land owned by others. As nomads, perhaps they did not think of land as a scarce resource, as may be suggested by the following example.

Thus, when Abram's and Lot's herdsmen came to strife, Abram and Lot settled their disputes amicably; Abram said, 'Is not the whole land before thee? Separate thyself, I pray thee, from me: if thou wilt take the left hand, then I will go to the right; or if thou depart to the right hand, then I will go to the left' (Gen. 13. 9). But on another occasion Abraham did not shrink from disputing rights over immovable property; however, the property right then at stake was a claim to water rather than to land. Abimelech had granted Abraham leave to roam on his territory and initially they had been on good terms: 'And Abimelech said, Behold, my land is before thee: dwell where it pleaseth thee' (Gen. 20: 15). Later their relationship became tense over rival claims to water: 'And Abraham reproved Abimelech because of a well of water, which Abimelech's servants had violently taken away' (Gen. 21: 25). Nor was this dispute ever settled; on the contrary, it festered beyond Abraham's lifetime. Isaac, Abraham's son, upheld his father's property rights: 'For all the wells which his father's servants had digged in the days of Abraham his father, the Philistines had stopped them, and filled them with earth' (Gen. 26: 15). And Isaac underscored his property claim: 'And Isaac digged again the wells of water, which they had digged in the days of Abraham his father; for the Philistines had stopped them after the death of Abraham: and he called their names after the names by which his father had called them' (Gen. 26: 18). Abraham and Isaac asserted through their actions that investment of labour could create a claim on immovable property.

As this shows, the essential features of the pre-Mosaic Israelite economy remained stable from the days of the patriarchs until the eve of Israelite entry into Canaan: Israelites mostly were nomadic shepherds and sometimes farmers, were precluded from owning land for investment, and valued water rights above land rights. After settling in Egypt, Israelites turned to farming; during forty years of wandering in the desert after the exodus from Egypt they were dishabituated from farming; and upon entry into Canaan once more were about to revert to farming. To prepare Israelites for this momentous change, Moses had to structure their economy anew.

## Mosaic economics

The Book of Genesis inspired Mosaic rules for the right to own property, for provision of welfare and for conduct of trade; the resulting economy was agricultural, stable and static. The construction Moses put on the right to own land and to receive welfare was drawn from the story of the creation and of the institution of the Sabbath.

The Book of Genesis explained that God put the world at humanity's disposal: 'And God said: Let us make man in our image, after our likeness: and let them have dominion over the fish of the sea, and over the fowl of the air, and over the cattle, and over all the earth, and over every creeping thing that creepeth upon the earth' (Gen. 1: 26). Moses expounded what were to be the implications of dominion over the Promised Land: God, as creator of the earth, was its true owner; Israelites were given the Promised Land as the Lord's stewards, for God had said, 'The land shall not be sold for ever: for the land is mine; for ye are strangers and sojourners with me' (Lev. 25: 23).

On entry into Canaan, land was divided between the tribes of Israel in proportion to their size: 'Unto these the land shall be divided for an inheritance according to the number of names. To many thou shalt give the more inheritance, and to few thou shalt give the less inheritance: to every one shall his inheritance be given according to those that were numbered of him' (Num. 26: 53–54). An individual family was allotted a farm sized to fit its needs. This entitlement was based on a family's membership in a particular tribe rather than on its own right; the property claim of a family ranked behind that of its tribe. There were implications for property rights.

As at the outset of Israelite tenure in Canaan every family would have been awarded a farm that was sized proportional to its needs; consequently, the wealth pyramid would have been flat. But inevitably, wealth differentials would have emerged over time, for two reasons.[2] One was the testamentary rule whereby an older son's portion was twice that of a younger son. This rule implied that the ratio between the largest and the smallest farms doubled with every generation. Another was crop failures. The smaller a farm, the smaller its reserves to tide it over with seed for next year's crop, and a smallholder who borrowed seed from his neighbours and defaulted on his loan was

---

2  'Archaeologists have corroborated gaps in wealth emerged over time. Israelite dwellings from the tenth century were sized similarly, those of the eighth century differently' (de Vaux 1961: 72–73).

consigned to slavery. Mosaic measures for distributing welfare and levelling wealth disparities were shaped by observance of the Sabbath (Ex. 20: 98–11; see also Ex. 23: 12):

> Six days you shall work and you shall do your tasks, but the seventh day is a Sabbath to the Lord your God. You shall do no task, you and your son and your daughter, your male slave and your slavegirl and your beast and your sojourner who is within your gates. For six days did the Lord make the heavens and the earth, the sea and all that is in it, and He rested on the seventh day.

Mosaic economics broadened the conception of the Sabbath. The semantics of 'Sabbath' is relevant here. In Hebrew, 'Sabbath' can be a verb or a noun: the noun means 'the day which marks a limit or a division', the verb means 'to cease working, to rest' (de Vaux 1961: 475–83). Moses widened the application of the Sabbath to economic arrangements.

After seven years, defaulters were released from debt slavery: 'If thou buy an Hebrew servant, six years shall he serve: and in the seventh he shall go out free for nothing' (Ex. 21: 2). Every seven days, work ceased; every seven years, fields were left untilled and debts cancelled (Ex. 21: 1–11); every seven cycles of seven years – the Jubilee Year – land reverted to original holders (Lev. 25: 10).[3] As a farmer did not own the land he farmed he did not have the right to sell it. Transfers of land such as there were – for example, after

---

3 'And you shall hallow the fiftieth year and call a release in the land to all its inhabitants.'

defaulting on debt – would be revoked in time, in keeping with the Lord's command: 'And in all the land of your holdings, you shall allow a redemption for the land' (Lev. 25: 23–24). A farmer's right to dispose of property was unrestricted, however, in respect of anything that came from his own labour. Examples were harvests or buildings.[4] The inalienability of land – as opposed to that of produce of labour – was in keeping with the approach Abraham had taken in his dispute with Abimelech. Notwithstanding literal compliance with Sabbath legislation would have been infeasible (the practical implications are outside the scope of this chapter), its egalitarian thrust was clear: to remit debt constituted a transfer of wealth from creditors to debtors, and to restore alienated land from the top income layers to the bottom income layers. In economic terms, Sabbath observance was tantamount to a package of income and welfare policies.

Moses encapsulated business ethics in his ban on usury. He invoked the Book of Genesis to define the right to own land and to shape distribution of welfare; however, he did not rely on the Book of Genesis to devise rules for fair trade. (Moses' ban on usury was formative for the economics of Christianity and of Islam; this will be reviewed presently.) By convention today, the term 'usury' has narrowed to

---

4   Residential property sales were exempt from restitution: 'And should a man sell a dwelling house in a walled town, its redemption shall be till the end of the year of its sale. A year its redemption shall be. And if it is not redeemed by the time a full year has elapsed for him, the house in the town that has a wall shall pass over irreversibly to its buyer for his generations. It shall not be released in the Jubilee' (Lev. 25: 29–30).

denote loans that charge interest. But in the era of Moses, 'usury' was a term applied to a much broader spectrum of exchanges, namely to any transaction where one party gained an advantage at the expense of another. A ban on usury aimed to secure fair economic relations between members of society.

Moses pronounced his ban on usury on four different occasions.[5] What he meant by it was difficult to interpret, however, for two reasons. Interpreters struggled to reconcile different terms Moses used to describe the concept; moreover, he seemed to contradict himself. Early in his leadership, Moses said, 'If you should lend money to My people, to the pauper among you, you shall not be to him like a creditor, you shall not impose interest on him' (Ex. 22: 24). Late in life, however, he said, 'You shall not exact interest from your brother, interest of silver, interest of food, or interest of anything that will bear interest. From the stranger you may exact interest but from your brother you shall not exact interest' (Deut. 23: 20–21). Moses appeared, at first blush, to have advocated a double standard: it would be illicit to charge interest from Israelites but licit to charge it from non-Israelites.[6] But what might have looked like ethnic discrimination in fact would have conduced to matching borrowers with loans appropriate to their needs, given economic circumstances of the time:

---

5  Ex. 22: 24–26; Lev. 25: 35–38; Deut. 23: 20–21; Deut. 24: 10–13.

6  'Usury, indeed, remains usury. But according to the correct interpretation of Deut. 23: 20, Jahwe will also bless this usury with success like all other ventures of the Israelite unless he practices it against brothers' (Weber 1952: 342).

Moses' discrimination between Israelites and strangers was commercial rather than ethnic. Israelite borrowers were farmers who paid interest out of shares from harvests; strangers, on the other hand, were long-distance traders who paid interest out of profit from commerce. As loans for agriculture and for commerce had different purposes, they had different levels of risk; and such would explain the reasoning why interest on loans to Israelites was illicit but that on loans to strangers licit.[7]

Moses banned interest on loans but that did not preclude him from approving of yields from investment. Indeed, he enacted rules governing how to assess the price for a farm.[8] In such transfers, Moses decreed, the purchaser acquired a claim on harvests rather than on land itself. In effect, the purchaser acquired a lease (Lev. 25: 15–16):

> According to the number of years after the jubilee thou shalt buy of thy neighbour, and according unto the number of years of the fruits he shall sell unto thee: According to the multitude of years thou shalt increase the price thereof, and according to the fewness of years thou shalt diminish the price of it: for according to the number of the years of the fruits doth he sell unto thee.

---

7  This conjecture is strengthened by Neufeld's observation: 'The word "Canaanite" and the word "trader" were for a long time synonymous names' (Neufeld 1955: 378). The Israelite ban on usury was at variance with Babylonian and Phoenician practices (1955: 359). For a fuller comparison, see Hejcl (1907).

8  Westbrook (1985) has shown correspondences between Israelite and Babylonian provisions.

## The absence of theology from contemporaneous economics

As already stated, the theological nature of Mosaic economics was unique, not only in the context of the Middle East but also when contrasted with contemporaneous economics in Sparta, Athens and Rome. For example, Moses followed certain Egyptian and Babylonian economic practices: Egyptians put ownership of land in the hands of a single authority – the pharaoh – and eschewed long-distance trade; Babylonians designated a day of rest in every lunar month, *shabbatu*, and celebrated the accession of a new king with remission of debt. Egyptians and Babylonians, however, did not link economic practices to theology.[9] To turn to Sparta, Athens and Rome, here economic reforms were also tied to land reform, but again these did not invoke religion. Contrasting case studies of economic reforms in Greece and Rome were provided by the Greek historian Plutarch (*c.* AD 46–120), who wrote biographies of the Spartan Lycurgus (*c.* 800 BC), the Athenian Solon (*c.* 600 BC) and the Roman Numa Pompilius (*c.* 600 BC). All three linked land reform to social reform.[10]

In Sparta, Lycurgus introduced reforms at a time when 'the city was heavily burdened with indigent and helpless people, and wealth was wholly concentrated in the hands

---

9 Babylonia's economic legislation did not invoke divine prescription. Sarna (1991: 274) wrote of the Codex Hammurabi: 'The text makes it perfectly clear that Hammurabi himself is the sole source of the legislation.'

10 All quotations from Plutarch's *Lives* are from Plutarch (1914).

of a few'. Lycurgus 'persuaded his fellow-citizens to make one parcel of all their territory and divide it up anew, and to live with one another on a basis of entire uniformity and equality in the means of subsistence'. Lycurgus discouraged long-distance trade and replaced gold coins with coins made of iron – too bulky to hide, too heavy to steal and worthless in exchange abroad. As foreign traders no longer had an incentive to visit Sparta on business, luxury 'died away of itself, and men of large possessions had no advantage over the poor, because their wealth found no public outlet'.

In Athens, Solon was rather less successful. Solon drafted a new constitution at a time when 'the common people were in debt to the rich. For they either tilled their lands for them ... or else they pledged their persons for debts and could be seized by their creditors'. Solon fell foul of his compatriots after it came to light that some of his friends had gotten wind that Solon would cancel debts; they used this information to buy up large tracts of land on loans on which they subsequently reneged without giving up their acquisitions. Solon's reputation never recovered: 'the rich were vexed because he took away their securities for debt, and the poor still more, because he did not redistribute the land, as they had expected, nor make all men equal and alike in their way of living, as Lycurgus did.' Solon had widened rather than narrowed the gap between rich and poor and lost the support of both, 'the former expecting to have equality based on worth and excellence, the latter on measure and count'.

In Rome, Numa Pompilius introduced equality of land holdings to encourage rightful conduct of social relations. Plutarch wrote:

> And indeed the city's territory was not extensive at first, but Romulus acquired most of it later with the spear. All this was distributed by Numa among the indigent citizens. He wished to remove the destitution which drives men to wrongdoing, and to turn the people to agriculture, that they might be subdued and softened along with the soil they tilled.

Plutarch showed why some land reforms succeeded when others failed: Lycurgus and Numa Pompilius had succeeded because they parcelled out land in equal lots; Solon had failed because he did not level differential land holdings. These three faced the same challenges as Moses – but not one made the case for reforms by invoking religion.

## Abrahamic economics versus Greek economics

In ancient Israel, economics was linked with theology, a legacy bequeathed to all three Abrahamic religions. In ancient Greece, on the other hand, theology did not enter economics. A comparison between the Abrahamic and Greek treatment of usury illustrates this distinction. Israelite and Greek lending practices had much in common; both had loans that were interest-free or interest-bearing; moreover, both disapproved of usury. In each Abrahamic faith, disapproval of usury was based on religion, but in ancient Greece otherwise. Let us see.

To turn to Judaism, the Judaic philosopher Philo Iudaeus (25 BC–AD 50) complied with Moses' ethical imperative whereby lending ought to be undertaken 'without expecting to receive anything beyond the principal. For in this way the poor will not become poorer, by being compelled to restore more than they received; nor will they who lent be doing iniquity if they only receive back what they lent.' [11]

To turn to Christianity, Jesus expounded Mosaic prescriptions on lending when he said, 'lend, hoping for nothing again' (Luke 6: 35). The Lord's Prayer included the following passage, 'And forgive us our sins; for we also forgive every one that is indebted to us' (Luke 11: 4, King James Version).

To turn to Islam, four suras in the Koran proscribed usury.[12] The condemnation of usurers in the Koran was stark: 'Those that live on usury shall rise before God like men whom Satan has demented by his touch' (Koran 2: 275). This ban was complemented by an admonition: 'That which you seek to increase by usury will not be blessed by God; but the alms you give for His sake shall be repaid to you many times over' (Koran 30: 38).

When Greeks reproved of usury, on the other hand, they did so without invoking religion: Solon outlawed loans secured with the borrower's person; Plato disapproved of 'much money-making by means of vulgar trading or usury

---

11  Philo, *On the Virtues*, pp. 83–84. In *The Works of Philo Judaeus* (trans. C. D. Yonge) (http://www.earlychristianwritings.com/yonge/book31.html).

12  Suras 2: 276–79; 3: 125; 4: 33; 159: 30–38.

or the fattening of gelded beasts' as 'of all three objects which concern every man, the concern for money, rightly directed, comes third and last'[13]; and Aristotle inveighed against interest: 'And this term interest, which means the birth of money from money, is applied to the breeding of money because the offspring resembles the parent. Wherefore of all modes of getting wealth this is the most unnatural.'[14] In sum, usury was condemned by Solon, Plato and Aristotle; as it was by Moses, Jesus and Muhammad – but only the latter invoked religion.

## The medieval and modern afterlife of Mosaic economics

In the history of economic thought from the Middle Ages to the Enlightenment and indeed to the present day, Mosaic economics has enjoyed a long and vigorous afterlife. A full exposition would be beyond the bounds of this chapter, so in the present context some representative examples must suffice. Thomas Aquinas (1225–74) treated Mosaic law at length in the *Summa theologiae,* where he quoted the Book of Genesis as the constitutive conception of the right to own property:

Moreover, this natural dominion of man over other creatures, which is competent to man in respect of his reason

---

13  Plato, *Laws,* 5. 743d–e (https://lucianofsamosata.info/demonax.info/doku .php?id=text:laws_-_plato5).

14  Aristotle, *Politics,* I. x. 1258b.

wherein God's image resides, is shown forth in man's creation (Genesis 1: 26) by the words: Let us make man to our image and likeness: and let him have dominion over the fishes of the sea, etc.[15]

In post-medieval Europe, Mosaic economics shaped how theologians, jurisprudents and sociologists came to understand the origin of the right to own land. The Enlightenment theologian Johann David Michaelis (1717–91) reviewed Moses' framing of property rights in his *Commentaries on the Laws of Moses*. He pointed out that Moses had decreed the inalienability of land (Michaelis 1814: 377):

In order to render this perpetual inalienability of lands more secure, and in a manner sacred, Moses adopted the principle of an Egyptian law, to which the Israelites had already been accustomed from their youth. In Egypt, the lands all belonged to the king, and the husbandmen were not the proprietors of the fields which they cultivated, but only farmers or tenants, who had to pay the king one-fifth of their produce, Gen XLVII. 20–25. In like manner, Moses declared God, who honoured the Israelites by calling himself their king, the sole land-proprietary of all the land of promise, in which he was about to settle them by his most special providence; while the people were to be merely his tenants, and without any right to alienate their possessions in perpetuity. Lev XXV.23.

---

15 *Summa theologiae* II. II. 66. a1 (http://www.newadvent.org/summa/3066 .htm).

Michaelis also was conscious of the social consequences of Mosaic economics (Michaelis 1814: 379–80):

> The advantages of this law, if sacredly observed, would have been very great. It served, in the first place, to perpetrate that equality among citizens, which Moses at first established, and which was suitable to the spirit of the democracy, by putting it out of the power of any flourishing citizen to become, by acquisition of exorbitant wealth, and the accumulation of extensive landed property, too formidable to the state, or, in other words, a little prince, whose influence would carry every thing before it. In the second place, it rendered it impossible that any Israelite could be born to absolute poverty, for every one had his hereditary land, and if that was sold, or he himself from poverty compelled to become a servant, at the coming of the year of jubilee, he recovered his property.

To turn to jurisprudence, William Blackstone (1723–80) in his *Commentaries on the Laws of England* cited the book of Genesis as the foundational source for deriving rights to own property (Blackstone 1765–69: II.i):

> There is nothing which so generally strikes the imagination, and engages the affections of mankind, as the right of property; or that sole and despotic dominion which one man claims and exercises over the external things of the world, in total exclusion of the right of any other individual in the universe. And yet there are very few, that will give themselves the trouble to consider the original

and foundation of this right ... In the beginning of the world, we are informed by holy writ, the all-bountiful Creator gave to man 'dominion over all the earth; and over the fish of the sea, and over the fowl of the air, and over every living thing that moveth upon the earth ... The earth, therefore, and all things therein, are the general property of all mankind, exclusive of other beings, from the immediate gift of the Creator. And, while the earth continued bare of inhabitants, it is reasonable to suppose that all was in common among them, and that every one took from the public stock to his own use as his immediate necessities required.

Blackstone was also conscious of the fine distinction between the right to property that resulted from individual effort as opposed to the right to property of land itself:

[B]odily labour, bestowed upon any subject which before lay in common to all men, is universally allowed to give the fairest and most reasonable title to an exclusive property therein ... And therefore the book of Genesis (the most venerable monument of antiquity, considered merely with a view to history) will furnish us with frequent instances of violent contentions concerning wells; the exclusive property of which appears to have been established in the first digger or occupant, even in such ground or places where the ground and herbage remained yet in common. Thus we find Abraham, who was but a sojourner, asserting his right to a well in the country of Abimelech, and exacting an oath for his security, 'because he had digged that well.' And Isaac, about ninety years afterwards, reclaimed this his father's property; and, after much contention with the Philistines, was suffered to enjoy it in peace. All this while the soil and pasture of the earth remained still in common as before, and open to every occupant.

To turn to twentieth-century sociology, Max Weber (1864–1920) in *Ancient Judaism* ascribed to Moses the seminal impact of constructing socio-economic norms derived from religion (Weber 1952: 254–55):

Unlike pre-exilic Israel Babylonia and Egypt knew no unified, religiously substructured ethic; Egypt had its doctrinal wisdom of life and the esoteric Book of the Dead, Babylonia had its collections of magically efficacious hymns and formulae, containing also ethical elements. In Israel this ethic was the product of the ethical Torah of the Levites continued for many generations, and of prophecy. Prophecy did not so much influence the content – which it rather accepted as given – rather it promoted systematic unification, by relating the people's life as a whole and the life of each individual to the fulfilment of Yahweh's positive commandments. Moreover, it eliminated the predominance of ritual in favour of ethics. In this the Levitical Torah gave its imprint to the content of the ethical commandments. Both jointly imparted to the ethic its simultaneously plebeian and systematic character.

Johann Michaelis, William Blackstone and Max Weber attested that Moses endowed Judeo-Christian culture with the earliest constructions of the right to own property. In economics – in contradistinction to theology, jurisprudence and sociology – there has been rather less engagement with the impact Moses had on conceptions of property rights. One would expect to find a reference to Moses in John Locke's *Second Treatise of Government* of 1689 in the chapter 'On property', but Moses was not among the many Biblical authorities – such as Adam, Noah and David – that he quoted. To infer that John Locke did not cite Moses because he overlooked him seems inconceivable, and perhaps Locke at the time might not have thought it opportune to point out too bluntly that his own stance on property rights was incompatible with that of Moses. In any event, Mosaic conceptions of property rights also did not feature in Adam Smith's *Lectures on Jurisprudence* of 1763, or in Joseph Schumpeter's *History of Economic Analysis* of 1954, or in Joseph Spengler's more recent *Origins of Economic Thought and Justice* (1980).

The relative neglect of Moses in economic literature is puzzling. It may be explained by the preoccupation of economists with the evolution of markets, for although the Bible had instances of the patriarchs in the process of buying and selling, it contained few references to markets as such. Indeed, as Maxime Rodinson (1973: lix–lx) pointed out, the Hebrew Bible did not have a term for 'markets'.[16]

---

16  Rodinson counted four references to a market, in the sense of stall-lined street, the term for which was derived from the Akkadian suq.

Jacob Neusner in his study of the economics of the Mishna pointed out that Mosaic notions of fairness in trade would have precluded a mercantile orientation of Israelite society.[17]

In recent decades interest in Moses has revived and there have been studies that raised awareness that the Hebrew Bible had implications also for the conduct of economics. Some examples follow. Dov Paris, in 'An economic look at the Old Testament' (Paris 1998), reviewed Judaic economics as a whole, even if he was silent regarding Moses' treatment of property rights. Barry Gordon's *The Economic Problem in Biblical and Patristic Thought* (1989) noted that Mosaic Israelites were landless and cited views on both sides of the argument that such implied the Mosaic economy was static rather than dynamic.[18] David Baker's *Tight Fists or Open Hands? Wealth and Poverty in Old Testament Law* (2009) has been the most thorough disquisition undertaken in recent decades on economic regulation in the Books of Moses; Baker's primary aim has been to promote an ethical dimension to public debate on economic issues. Tomáš Sedláček's *Economics of Good and Evil* (2011) noted that Old Testament eschatology understood history as a temporal sequence that was linear rather than

---

17  The Mishnah's 'framers took for granted that money formed a commodity for barter, and that all forms of profit – all forms! – constituted nothing other than "usury" that Scripture had condemned' (Neusner 1990: 93).

18  'It cannot be said that after Leviticus and Deuteronomy the face of the Law was set unequivocally against the economic development of Israel. However, it may be that the Law helped structure the economy so that certain types of growth were more likely to occur than others' (Gordon 1989: 18–19).

cyclical, which, he inferred, fostered attitudes conducive to economic growth. Edd Noell's 'Theonomy and economic institutions' (2014) reviewed the scope for implementing Mosaic economics in practice. Notably, only two scholars in this group, Barry Gordon and Edd Noell, came to their subject from economics, while the author of the most comprehensive review of economics in the Old Testament, David Baker, is a theologian.

## Conclusion

As we have seen, Israelite economic practices before and after Moses differed in key respects. Pre-Moses, Israelites switched between shepherding and farming, did not invest in land, and stored wealth in mobile goods. On entry into Canaan, a sedentary economy superseded a nomadic economy; Moses laid down economic norms that governed rights to land ownership, welfare and trade. Property rights were framed by the divine pronouncement, 'Mine is the Land, says the Lord'; welfare policies were inspired by the institution of the Sabbath. Many particulars of Mosaic economics – such as granting the right to own land to collectives rather than to individuals – were in keeping with those of contemporaneous societies in Greece and Rome at corresponding stages of development, and, as such, Mosaic property rights were representative of an intermediate phase in the evolution of property rights, a stage where property came to be owned by a collective rather than by an individual. However, Moses was unique in that he based economic norms on theology, which innovation set him apart from Egyptian and Babylonian precursors and from contemporaneous Greeks and Romans, and which legacy has remained a defining characteristic of economic conceptions in all three Abrahamic religions. The seminal impact of Mosaic economics has long been acknowledged in theology, jurisprudence and sociology; but it still awaits recognition in economics. It has been commonplace to assume economic thinking originated in ancient Greece rather than in ancient Israel. Arguably, however, Moses was the first normative economist in Judeo-Christian culture.

# 4 MUHAMMAD'S CONCEPTION OF PROPERTY AS A BUNDLE OF RIGHTS

Benedikt Koehler

## The *waqf*

*Waqf*s are Islamic institutions that provide welfare. Institutional economists and historians have been studying *waqf*s for three reasons, two of which are of interest to historians while the third relates to current policy issues. First, philanthropy in medieval Islam was of a scale and range unprecedented in Middle Eastern and European history; second, the legal structure of the *waqf* conceivably inspired common law trusts. These two historical facts bear on a third issue, one that is topical today, namely why civil society in Islamic countries seems stagnant and what remedy might act as agent of change. *Waqf*s in many Islamic countries have been nationalised over the course of the twentieth century – a policy that, as this article shows, not only contravenes the original principles of the *waqf* but has thereby also enfeebled a traditional hub of civil society in Islam. Deliberations on how to promote civil society in Islam should rightly consider the contribution that *waqf*s made to civil society in Islam.

A conception of property as a bundle of rights crystallised in the *waqf*, I argue, from the precedents for provision of welfare set by Muhammad. I reject the claim that *waqf*s from the outset represented an assimilation of pre-existing legal cultures in Islam's enlarged empire, and I aver that the conduit for transmitting the template of *waqf*s to England may have been the Knights Templar and Franciscan friars. My argumentation bears on policy issues in Islamic societies today, in two respects: restoring Muhammad's original intent would reverse state control over *waqf*s; and it would thereby widen the scope for pluralist welfare provision that was manifest in the early history of Islam.

## *Background to waqfs and welfare*

A word on how a *waqf* is framed. A legal instrument constituting a *waqf* binds three parties: a donor, a manager and beneficiaries. Accordingly, the donor passes assets to the *waqf*; a manager taking control of these assets must do so at arm's length from the donor; and the purpose to which these assets are put is defined in advance. Other determinations include particulars such as the manager's salary, complaints procedures and what should happen in case the original purpose of the *waqf* falls away (the income never reverts to the donor and, as a general rule, is applied to poor relief). By way of example, a typical *waqf* in early Islam may have consisted of a distinct asset (say, an orchard), producing income (say, a harvest), applied to a defined purpose (say, feeding orphans).

Poor relief is a core Islamic obligation, and the Koran specifies how it should be funded, namely through *zakat*, a levy on wealth. On the other hand, the Koran makes no mention of *waqf*s; at first blush, therefore, *waqf*s do not seem intrinsic to Islam. A consequential inference, that *waqf*s came into being only long after the death of Muhammad in 632, is further strengthened by certain facts, specifically that *waqf*s first appeared in legal literature in 818 (in a tract by Yayha ibn Adam (Hennigan 2004: 50)), and the oldest inscription on a building documenting ownership by a *waqf* is dated to the tenth century (Cahen 1961: 40). The timing of the first *waqf*s – whether they are a Muhammadan or a post-Muhammadan innovation – is an issue of some consequence, because if *waqf*s only came into being long after Muhammad's lifetime they are hardly essential to the ethos of Islam. This paper settles the issue of the moment in history when *waqf*s appeared: Muhammad introduced the conception of property as a bundle of rights when he disposed of conquered lands around Khaybar, an oasis north of Medin. Moreover, *waqf*s cannot be deemed to be derived from non-Islamic precursors because antecedent models of welfare provision did not treat property as a bundle of rights. We first turn to how public welfare was delivered before the advent of Islam.

## *Precursors to waqfs*

Private philanthropy was already practised long before the advent of Islam. The world's earliest record of a charitable endowment, wherein land was gifted to yield income for a temple, may be a Babylonian legal deed dated to *c.* 1,300 BC (Laum 1914: 207–9). The Babylonian template for charitable giving remained substantially unchanged throughout Roman and Byzantine history: assets, usually dedicated to maintaining religious institutions (or ancillary functions, such as administering cemeteries), were vested in a public authority, either the state or the church (Hennigan 2004: 52–53). There was an exception, ancient Persia, where benefactors were free to appoint administrators unaffiliated to a church or state authority.[19] We will return to the implications of ring-fencing an endowment from control by state or church, because this legal provision has consequences of great moment; but for now note only that the Persian antecedent is the best fit with a *waqf.* We now turn to public charity as practised in Muhammad's Medina.

## The overlap of zakat and waqfs

It is not obvious why the Koran could endorse *zakat* but not *waqf*s. However, as the economic historian Claude Cahen (1961: 45) has shown, conflating financial terms was not uncommon in early Islam. Cahen used in illustration the two Islamic taxes on non-believers, *jizya* and *kharaj*. Only one of these, *jizya*, is mentioned by the Koran, whereas *kharaj* was only introduced following Muslim occupation of regions outside Arabia, several years after Muhammad had died; hence, arguably, *kharaj* was superimposed on a Koranic

---

19 Furthermore, a distinction was drawn between the endowment's principal and usufruct (Perikhanian 1983).

guideline. But Cahen resolved this ostensible inconsistency: *jizya* is a levy on movable assets (say, a herd), and *kharaj* is a levy on a fixed asset (say, a farm). Thus, the two taxes share an identical rationale – the taxation of non-believers – and differ only in the basis of the assessment.

There is an obvious analogy with *zakat* and *waqf*s: they share the same purpose – provision of welfare – and differ in that *zakat* is based on tax levied on movable assets, whereas a *waqf* earns rents from property in its possession; *zakat* is managed within the public sector, *waqfs* are outside the public sector. What may seem an arcane minutia of fiscal procedure – which asset base is used to yield income – had important ramifications for the provision of public welfare. *Zakat* was levied on movable wealth (say, a herd) that fluctuated from one year to the next; movable assets *in extremis* could disappear altogether, and, consequently, so could tax yields. *Waqf*s, on the other hand, took possession of a fixed asset (say, a building) with a more predictable revenue flow. *Zakat*, therefore, was a less dependable tool for drafting a long-term budget, whereas a *waqf*, through control of assets, was thus equipped to commit to welfare provision over several budget periods.

We now track back in time to Medina in the days of Muhammad, to the origin of the first *waqf*s, and how in practice they came to be differentiated from *zakat*.

## Introduction of *waqfs* by Muhammad

In Medina, charitable endowments were a feature of civic life even before Muhammad arrived there. A certain Al Bar had died months before Muhammad settled in Medina and had settled a portion of his estate on charity. Muhammad not only raised no objection; on the contrary, he endorsed this bequest. Thus Al Bar was 'the first to will away a third of his wealth and the Messenger of God allowed it' (Ibn Sa'd 2013: 482). Muhammad acquired personal experience of handling endowments shortly after the Battle of Uhud (in 625) when Muqairiq, a Jewish warrior in Muhammad's armed forces who was fatally wounded in the battle, bequeathed to the Prophet seven properties with the proviso he put these to use for the expansion of Islam.

The Arab Islamic scholar Ibn Sa'd describes how Muhammad managed this endowment. Muhammad once spotted his grandson Hassan eating fruit from a tree that had been given over to provide food for the poor (since no other landed endowments in Medina are ever mentioned, this orchard must have been part of Muqairiq's bequest). Muhammad scooped the fruit from the boy's mouth and scolded him, 'Don't you know you are not to eat *sadaka*?' (Ibn Sa'd 2012: 122; Gil 1998: 128). (The term *sadaka* – also *sadaqa* – is a synonym for *zakat*.) Thus, Muqairiq's bequest was of great moment in the evolution of *waqf*s: Muhammad was now in a position to fund *zakat* through charging rent on a capital asset, and a mechanism for administering a *waqf* was in place. Two aspects of this *hadith* stand out: first, Muhammad was conversant with reserving an orchard to provide welfare, and, second, Muhammad applied the term *sadaka* to what was in fact a *waqf*. Muhammad saw no need for new nomenclature to distinguish between *zakat* and *waqf*.

Muqairiq's bequest gave Muhammad a blueprint for administering a *waqf*, and his next step was to scale up how this concept was applied. This occurred following the conquest of Khaybar in 628 (four years before Muhammad died). Previously, income from raids consisted exclusively of windfalls; now, Muhammad came into possession of extensive agricultural estates. The campaign against Khaybar marked a new phase in Muhammad's bid for recognition as pan-Arabian leader; moreover, the finances of Muhammad's polity were transformed when Khaybar and its environs were brought under his control. Tenants of farms in and near Khaybar were not evicted; instead, Muhammad permitted them to remain on their land but imposed on them an annual tribute, equivalent to 50 per cent of their harvests. Muhammad, as commander-in-chief entitled to one fifth of any booty, became the recipient of a very large recurring income stream; his annual income was higher than that of any other Arab of the time.[20]

Muhammad simultaneously awarded grants of lands to his Companions, but attached the condition that they apply the proceeds from land to the public welfare. The narrative of events by Ibn Sa'd shows that the term *sadaka* was still used interchangeably with *waqf* (Ibn Sa'd 2013: 280):

Umar got some land at Khaybar and went to the Prophet and he gave him command in it. He said, 'I got land in

---

20 Following the conquest of Khaybar, Muhammad drew annual rents of 1.5m gold franks, according to an estimate by Leone Caetani (1907: 47).

> Khaybar and I did not get any property dearer to me than it. What do you command me to do with it?' He said: 'If you wish, make it a *waqf* and give it as *sadaqa*.' Umar gave it as *sadaqa* ... the first *sadaqa* given in Islam were the fruits of the *sadaqa* of Umar ibn al Khattab.

A distinction was drawn between property rights over a capital asset and property rights over the yield from that asset. Fixed assets were owned by a *waqf*, but income flows were due to beneficiaries; the *waqf* was the legal entity constituted to administer this scheme. Muhammad thus complied with the Koranic injunction to provide charity, but he did so in a new way, namely by using capital assets and ring-fencing them from control by a secular or religious authority. Previously, assets reserved for the provision of welfare had always been in the hands of a secular or religious authority, but henceforth they were vested in an independent, distinct legal entity. Umar and other Companions had title to physical assets, but beneficiaries had claims over yields from assets: thus, at that very moment the conception of property as a bundle of rights had come into being. A transition in jurisprudence which had proceeded in several stages had now run its course. Muqairiq, who gifted a benefaction to the Prophet as head of the community, had complied with traditional philanthropic practice since he did not impose legal constraints on Muhammad; but after Khaybar, Muhammad broke new ground by granting to his Companions legal title over land while constraining how they could use income derived from it and making the distribution of benefits subject to legal oversight.

The novelty of Muhammad's approach is thrown into relief by a recapitulation of traditional models of delivering welfare. Endowments in the era lasting from the Babylonian empire to the Byzantine empire were administered by state or church authorities, and no institutional checks and balances afforded protection against these authorities absorbing and consolidating endowments. Administrators of *waqf*s, on the other hand, were independent of church or state. This key difference explains why before the advent of Islam the state or the church absorbed philanthropic institutions, whereas the legal structure of *waqf*s, where administrators were at arm's length from church and state, safeguarded their independence. By creating a vehicle for a civic philanthropy that was legally autonomous, Muhammad and his Companions had in effect arrived at a conception of property as a bundle of rights; and the independent status of *waqf* administrators, I submit, explains why the philanthropic sector in Islam spawned creativity surpassing that of its predecessors. (Fixing the timing of the first *waqf*s has the collateral implication of settling the question whether Islamic welfare provision imitated Persian models: this hypothesis is disproved because by the time Islam incorporated Persia the template for *waqf*s was already in place.)

## Reliability of sources

Before we leave Arabia and turn our attention to England, and to how trusts came into being there, we should pause for a moment and deal with two questions that recur in the literature pertinent to the study of *waqf*s. The first concerns the reliability of *hadith*s that narrate the evolution of *waqf*s, the second what was the true motivation of benefactors of *waqf*s. *Hadith*s, some claim, are unreliable as historical evidence, because for generations they were passed on only orally and were therefore liable to distortions. This assertion, however, was refuted long ago by Aloys Sprenger (1856a–c). As to the motivation of benefactors, there are doubts about what, if not charity, might explain why *waqf*s came into being. An intuitive putative motivation put forward is pecuniary considerations. One might question, however, the merit of this hypothesis. If acquisition of personal wealth had been uppermost in the mind of Muhammad and his Companions, nothing would have prevented them from owning the lands around Khaybar outright. A closer fit between intentions and outcomes is provided by the Koran, which teaches that the provision of charity is an essential aspect of Islam. 'Islamic charity', according to Yaacov Lev (2005: 144), 'was a sacred charity, a form of worship, rather than a form of altruistic behaviour'. A vivid illustration of how fundamental to early Islam this virtue was is offered by another of Ibn Sa'd's *hadith*s. Once, when one of Muhammad's Companions descried an old man beset with dementia suffering from neglect by his family, he upbraided the family and compelled them to serve the old man the most delicious and costly dish they could afford; when they objected that 'he does not know what he is eating' and complained about the expense, they were cut short with a curt rebuke: 'but Allah knows' (Ibn Sa'd 2012: 227). In this *hadith* the motivation for endowing *waqf*s shines through; Islamic philanthropy can be comprehensively explained by the core values of Islam.

## The evolution of trusts and corporations in Christendom

In medieval England, the conception of property as a bundle of rights again emerged, in common law, in the form of trusts. A study of the statutes of one of Europe's earliest instances of trusts – those of Merton College, Oxford, endowed in 1264 – has concluded: 'Were the Merton documents written in Arabic, rather than Latin, the statutes could surely be accepted as a *waqf* instrument' (Gaudiosi 1988: 1254–55). Such parallels could be dismissed as spurious – how could lawyers in England have had knowledge of *waqf*s? I now turn to the question of how the jurisprudential expertise required to create *waqf*s could have been acquired in Europe.

Islamic law extended the privilege of endowing *waqf*s to non-Muslims, including Christians in Jerusalem. An early Islamic legal manual stated (Gil 1984: 157)[21]:

> If a Christian makes his land or his house *waqf* and prescribes that their revenue be spent for repairs in Jerusalem or to buy oil for its lamps or any (other) of its needs (it is permitted) ... also, Jews have in this respect the same rights as the Christians.

---

21  This manual, by Al-Khassaf, is dated to *c.* 893.

Christians must have made use of this right, since according to Ibn Sa'd (1997: 221), 'Umar II said that the *waqf* of a *dhimmi* who leaves a place of worship as a *waqf* from his property for the Christians or Jews is allowed'. Christians were exposed to Islamic philanthropy also as beneficiaries. The Omayyad caliph Abd al Malik instructed his all-powerful minister Hajjaj ibn Yusuf to transfer funds to enable Nestorians (a Christian sect) to build a monastery; the Abbasid caliph Harun al Rashid made a donation for building a Nestorian monastery in Baghdad (Pahlitzsch 2009: 146–47). A sixteenth-century legal deed that has come down to us documents a Muslim judge ascertaining the compliance of deeds of a *waqf* endowed by a Christian lady (Amin 1975). It follows that the mechanism of *waqf*s was known to Christians in the Middle East, and benefactions crossed denominational lines.

Next, we follow the trail by which this institutional expertise might have migrated to England.

Jerusalem was a gateway between Christendom and Islam. Two organisations – the Knights Templar and Franciscan friars – had a sizeable presence in both Jerusalem and England. The evolution of trusts in England owed much to them in particular. The benefactor of Merton College, Walter de Merton, had close ties to the Knights Templar; Franciscan friars, according to the legal historian Frederick Maitland (1894), were conspicuous as plaintiffs in cases leading to the endowment of trusts. Precedential actions for trusts were instigated by an official linked to the Knights Templar and by Franciscan friars rather than by other parties. Such facts constitute circumstantial evidence, which, however, falls short of ir-refutable evidence; but even if circumstantial evidence is not tantamount to proof, it should be noted that no other plausible explanation for the emergence of trusts has ever been produced.

Before I move on to modern policy ramifications, a brief review of the argument of this article up to this point is in order. I argue that *waqf*s originated in provisions made by Muhammad, and that, proceeding from these provisions, there emerged in early Islam an innovative legal concep-tion of property, namely property as a bundle of rights. Placing the origins of *waqf*s in Muhammad's lifetime by implication supports the assertion that early Islam was a catalyst for the self-sustaining evolution of formative in-stitutions of civil society in sectors such as education and health. A corollary of the assertion that *waqf*s originated in Muhammad's policy measures is that claims that civil society in Islam was stagnant from the outset are unten-able. These findings have implications for present-day pol-icies towards *waqf*s in Islamic societies.

## Implications for policy today

Civil society in the West is dynamic, but in the Islamic East, quiescent. One of the reasons for this divergence is thought to lie in the different pathways of evolution of *waqf*s and trusts; *waqf*s remained the dominant model of welfare provision in medieval Islam while in contempo-raneous Europe trusts evolved into corporations, which proved a far more malleable instrument for combining civic initiatives.[22] It is true that trusts were precursors of corporations, the jurisprudential frame for which, according to John Dewey (1926), appeared when in 1252 the Vatican issued the legal definition of a *universitas* as an entity with rights and duties distinct from those of its members.[23] The creation of the *universitas* marked a fork in the road from whence Europe progressed towards new forms of legal entities, whereas Islam did not. However, empirics demonstrate that *waqf*s also proliferated, flourished and expanded for many centuries, even until the modern era, and their decline has been comparatively recent. Thus, we need to track back once more to Medina in the seventh century to discover the source of the vitality of *waqf*s.

Broadening the purposes of *waqf*s began almost at once, and as time went on *waqf*s became an important feature of civic life in Islam. Muhammad encouraged reserving a third of bequests to charity (Ibn Hanbal 2012, vol. 2, *hadith* 1440). On a different occasion he instructed another Companion, Othman, to buy a well and give it over to free use (Ibn Hanbal 2012, vol. 1, *hadith*s 511, 545). Abu Bakr, the first caliph, created a *waqf* for the benefit of his descendants; Umar, the second caliph, passed his entitlement to one-fifth of the booty following the conquest of Egypt to a *waqf* (Gil 1998: 128). Benefactors were inventive in their

---

22 'The waqf became Islam's main organizational form for providing social services at a time when western Europe started to use the corporation to many of the same ends' (Kuran 2005: 802).

23 'For example, the "fiction" theory of the personality of corporate bodies, or universitates, was promulgated if not originated, by Pope Innocent IV (1243–1254)' (Dewey 1926: 665).

choice of dedicated purposes; mosques, schools, hospitals, homes for the aged were but a few of the proliferating beneficiaries of *waqf*s. Nor were benefactions of *waqf*s the preserve of Islam's male elite; donors came from every section of society (Hoexter 1998: 478). Women in particular were conspicuous in the history of *waqf*s from the first: Umar appointed as manager of the first *waqf* his daughter, Hafsa (Hennigan 2004: 162); and between 20 and 50 per cent of all medieval *waqf*s are estimated to have been endowed by women (Hoexter 1998: 478). A prominent example in the sixteenth century was Roxelana, wife of the sultan Suleiman the Magnificent, who endowed a Jerusalem *waqf* funded by the revenues of 26 villages (Kuran 2001: 849). Nor did this tradition cease after the Middle Ages; *waqf*s in Islamic societies were a significant economic sector until relatively recently. In Egypt, by the time of the Ottoman conquest, virtually all the buildings in Cairo were *waqf*s (Behrens-Abouseif 1994: 145). In Istanbul in the eighteenth century, soup kitchens daily served some 30,000 meals; on the eve of the foundation of the Republic of Turkey in 1923, *waqf*s owned three-quarters of arable land in the country (Kuran 2001: 849–50).

## Summary

*Waqf*s originated in the era of Muhammad rather than at a later stage of Islamic history. Moreover, *waqf*s do not serve as an example of institutional stagnation in Islam, contrasting with European dynamism, for two reasons: first, Europeans were exposed to *waqf*s in Jerusalem, where they were authorised to introduce them, and in Europe the first trusts replicated the very structure of *waqf*s; and second, *waqf*s outgrew their initial scale, and even up to the recent past were a malleable instrument for welfare provision. It follows, therefore, that *waqfs* – by proliferation of purpose, range of social strata involved and assets under management – were in every respect suggestive of a civil society capable of exploiting potential institutional creativity.

*Waqf*s in the nineteenth and twentieth centuries came under state control; and today in many Islamic countries governmental departments are dedicated to central management of *waqf*s.[24] The dynamic inherent in *waqf*s at their origin, whereby a bundle of rights could be assigned to autonomous institutions, thus atrophied, and *waqf*s suffered the fate of charitable foundations in pre-Islamic eras, namely to be dissolved by church or state authorities. What has been stifling a vibrant civil society in Islamic societies, I submit, has not been the presence of *waqf*s but, on the contrary, their disappearance. To privatise *waqf*s, by implication, would be a policy prescription strengthening the civil sector and reigniting the institutional dynamic once set in motion by Muhammad.

---

24 The legal standing of waqfs in French colonies in the nineteenth century was withdrawn, for example by a 'Rule against Perpetuities' (Hennigan 2004: 186). Elsewhere, for example in Turkey shortly after birth of the republic, the assets of waqfs were nationalised.

# 5 THE ECONOMICS OF PROPERTY RIGHTS IN EARLY AND MEDIEVAL CHRISTIANITY

Benedikt Koehler

The object of this essay is to review the economics of property rights that evolved in early and medieval Christianity. While this intellectual heritage was reflected in the work of John Locke and of Pope Benedict XVI, the doctrines of early Christianity have rarely featured on the agenda of economists. This is unsurprising, given that Joseph Schumpeter, Jacob Viner and Frank Knight, three authoritative economists, claimed that no economics at all could be extracted from the teaching of early and medieval Christianity. Schumpeter (1954: 72) explained, 'the Christian Church did not aim at social reform in any sense other than that of moral reform of individual behaviour ... The How and Why of economic mechanisms were *then* of no interest either to its leaders or to its writers.' Jacob Viner (1978: 14), too, detected in early Christianity an absence of pragmatic attitudes to societal relations, claiming '[t]he early Christian ideal was in the political field anarchic in character and in the economic field communistic'. Frank Knight asserted '[t]he freedom and equality for which religion has stood have been purely spiritual, never material.

For such reasons, the history of Christianity does not seem to me to point to the direction of rational ethical and social idealism' (Knight and Merriam 1947: 190).

These assessments, I argue, overlook the fact that Christianity pioneered conceptions of property rights and of poor relief. I review this evolution in the work of Tertullian in Carthage (*c.*155–*c.*240), Ambrose of Milan (*c.*340–*c.*397) and John Chrysostomos in Constantinople (347–407). I then turn to conceptions of property rights that emerged from a dispute instigated by Francis of Assisi (1181/2–1226) and settled by Pope John XXII (1244–1334).

## Public munificence in Roman antiquity

A comparison with welfare provision in Roman antiquity clarifies the picture of changes wrought by early Christianity. True, ancient Rome left a rich legacy of benefactions such as amphitheatres and temples that are among the most impressive remains of Roman architecture. Moreover, many were financed by Romans of means, whose donations instilled civic pride and raised the quality of life of all sections of society. Romans had a word for such generosity, *liberalitas*, denoting a combination of civic virtue and personal excellence that redounded to a benefactor's prestige. The practice of *liberalitas* was a marker of a benefactor's social status; elite Romans vied to outdo each other through endowments and banquets that spread favours on as grand a scale as resources would allow. For example, Julius Caesar, ever eager to dazzle his compatriots, in 46 BC celebrated a triumph with a feast set for 22,000 tables.

Roman private munificence improved public services and facilities, but the motivation for *liberalitas* was to exalt a benefactor's status. The notion that indigence might generate a legitimate claim to succour never entered into a donor's deliberations: poor relief, a core purpose of welfare, never evolved in Roman philanthropy.

This assertion invites challenge: after all, Roman emperors laid on for the people of Rome *panem et circenses* ('bread and games'), a practice regarded as an underpinning of Rome's social contract. Indeed, the roots of food support reached deep into Rome's history: in 123 BC, wheat prices were capped; in 58 BC, there began free distribution of wheat, the *annona*.[1] By the time Caesar came to power in 49 BC, the distribution list had swollen to 320,000, a figure which he trimmed back to 150,000, but which during the reign of Augustus (27 BC – AD 14) soon crept up again to 200,000. But, to be clear, the *annona* constituted a reward for political partisans; eligibility for it did not depend on means testing; moreover, the *annona* was not systematically adopted across the empire. It was not, therefore, poor relief as such.

The closest Romans came to a model of welfare spending was the *collegia tenuirum*, societies whose members paid a subscription that covered their burial expenses (Uhlhorn 1883: 21). In essence, *collegia* were collectives whose members distributed benefactions among themselves; in other words, they were mutual societies. *Collegia* were constituted through legal licences, which were

---

1 The *annona* is described comprehensively in van Berchem (1939).

difficult to obtain because the authorities were wary of civic associations that might incubate conspiracies. Hence, *collegia* were rare. Roman philanthropy had a blind spot: to amuse the masses, it built the Colosseum; but hospitals were unknown.

Roman indifference to poor relief was linked to conceptions of property rights. According to Cicero's treatise *De Officiis*, written in 44 BC, private property dated from the moment social conventions supplanted the state of nature when it came about through a first-mover advantage, *vetere occupatione* ('long occupancy').[2] Inequality in wealth, however capricious, was taken as a given, and nowhere did Cicero state that property imposed an obligation on owners to dole out relief for those who were less fortunate. On the contrary, Cicero decried food subsidies because they induced idleness.[3]

The Romans deemed efforts aiming at material betterment vulgar; the poet Ovid castigated the urge to own as *amor sceleratus habendi* ('loving to have is wretched' (Anderson 1997: 48)). They were indifferent to the plight of the poor since property ownership did not entail an obligation to care for them; on the contrary, the dramatist Plautus has a stage character voice sentiments about the plight of the poor that are positively callous: 'He does the beggar

2   'Sunt autem privata nulla natura, sed aut vetere occupatione' (Cicero 1913: 22).

3   'Caius Gracchus moved his grain law: a delightful business for the plebs. For it generously provided sustenance free of toil, patriots, by contrast, fought back, because that the plebs would be seduced from the ways of hard work and become slothful, and they saw that the treasury would be drained dry' (Cicero 2006: 103).

but a bad service who gives him meat and drink; for what he gives is lost, and the life of the poor is but prolonged to their own misery' (quoted by Uhlhorn 1883: 5).

I now turn to innovations in conceptions of welfare provision following the rise of Christianity.

## Christian welfare in Carthage, Milan and Constantinople

Christians adopted approaches to welfare that were new to Roman eyes. The very first community of Christians, in first-century Jerusalem, hosted free communal meals; deacons were appointed to oversee distribution of the common fund that had been endowed by wealthy members of the congregation though property sales (Acts 4–6). Soon, Christian congregations were springing up elsewhere; three prominent communities of the first four centuries AD were those of Carthage, Milan and Constantinople. In each of these cities, the conditions from which Christianity emerged were radically different: Tertullian's Carthage was a provincial city under Roman occupation and Christians had no say in how the city was run; Ambrose's Milan was a capital city in the Italian heartland of the empire where Christians were bidding for supremacy over pagans; and Chrysostomos in Constantinople worked in a capital city founded by an emperor, Constantine, who had turned his back on Rome and on paganism. In each of these locations, particulars of time and place determined how Christians conceived of poor relief and the right to own property.

## Tertullian in Carthage

The known facts about Tertullian are few but salient: he was born in Carthage, his father was a Roman soldier, and he was a convert from paganism. But each fact sheds light on Tertullian's approach to poor relief. Carthage, a metropolis once razed to the ground by Romans, by the second century AD was once more one of the largest ports of the Mediterranean because north Africa was Rome's main supplier of grain. Christianity arrived in Carthage from Alexandria but, geographically and economically, Rome mattered more. In Alexandria, Church Fathers wrote in Greek; the Carthaginian Tertullian was the first Church Father who wrote in Latin.

Tertullian was son of a father who served in the Roman army and would have understood only too well that the authorities would be alert to potential insurrections, and that he therefore needed to allay suspicions that his congregation might be a breeding ground for conspiracies. His *Apology*, written in 197 AD, addressed these very concerns, asserting that Christians were law-abiding subjects outside the fray of political factions and considered themselves citizens of the world.[4] Tertullian underscored the characterisation of the essentially docile nature of the *corpus Christianorum*, as he named his quaint community, through his description of the Christian approach to property and welfare (Tertullian 1931: 175–77):

---

4   '[N]ec ulla magis res aliena quam publica. Unam omnium rempublicam agnoscimus mundum' (Tertullian 1931: 172).

Even if there is a chest of a sort, it is not made up of money paid in entrance-fees, as if religion were a matter of contract. Every man once a month brings some coin – or whatever he wishes, and only if he does wish, and if he can; for nobody is compelled; it is a voluntary offering. You might call them the trust funds of piety [*deposita pietatis*]. For they are not spent upon banquets nor drinking parties nor thankless eating-houses; but to feed the poor and to bury them, for boys and girls who lack property and parents, and then for slaves grown old and shipwrecked mariners; and any who may be in mines, islands or prisons, provided that it is for the sake of God's school, become the pensioners of their confession [*alumni confessionis*].

Tertullian bracketed his community's income, *deposita pietatis*, with corresponding spending on beneficiaries, *alumni confessionis*. This practice marked key differences between Christians and pagans: Christians admitted members without asking for a subscription and widened benefits beyond the confines of the community. The direction towards which Christians were channelling their energies may have seemed innocuous enough to Romans of the time, but Charles Guignebert, Tertullian's biographer, has indicated how radical a break this was: 'c'est la fraternité chrétienne qui prend la place du patriotisme romain' (Guignebert 1901: 180). Already, then, Christianity was on the pathway to a model of society where, according to Andrea Giardina (2007: 768), 'poverty assumed a central position, in the collective imagination as in the redistribution of wealth'. Tertullian's *Apology* may have dispelled fears of an emerging potential threat to Roman rule, but in the long run the practices Tertullian described were to prove more disruptive of the pagan model for ordering society than any insurrection in Carthage ever could have been. But pagan ears were uncomprehending.

## Constantine the Great and Ambrose of Milan

In third-century Carthage, Christians were under pressure from pagans, but this situation had reversed by the time Ambrose became bishop in Milan. A turning point had occurred during the reign of the emperor Constantine (*c.* 272–337). A set of interlinking policies that transformed Christianity from an informal civic association into a quasi-public institution were a catalyst for conceptions of welfare and property rights that were to appear in the writings of Ambrose.

Constantine used law and economics to strengthen the institutional standing of Christianity. He revoked the right of plaintiffs to appeal a bishop's court ruling in another court where the judge was a pagan; this measure placed pagan and clerical judges on an equal footing. Constantine also paved the way for new approaches to property rights through his church-building programme. When Constantine assumed power, Rome, the capital, was crowded with pagan temples of imposing dimensions. Christian churches, on the other hand, for the most part were repurposed private abodes, barely recognisable as churches from the outside and, compared with pagan temples, altogether unprepossessing. In 312 Constantine endowed the Lateran Basilica, which, by providing space for up to 3,000 worshippers, surpassed the capacity of house churches by several orders of magnitude. Constantine might have thought it impolitic to situate a church adjacent to a temple, but finding a suitable location for a building of that size in the centre of Rome would have been hard in any event. Constantine had to settle for giving over a portion of the gardens of his private residence, and although the message the Lateran Basilica proclaimed by its size was clear enough, still, unlike a pagan temple, it was indisputably situated in the private sector and not the public sector, demonstrating that, even if Christianity was favoured by the emperor, it remained a private, not a public, institution. Richard Krautheimer, the Berkeley art historian, has pointed out the significance of Constantine's gift also in respect of property rights (Krautheimer 1983: 30):

> The Lateran basilica was his private foundation, financed from the privy purse and donated by him to the Christian community of Rome. Whether in the deed of gift the recipient named was the *corpus Christianorum Romae*, the *catholicae (ecclesiae) venerabile consilium*, or possibly the bishop matters little. In any event it was, in 312–13 certainly, a legal body or an individual, set apart from any official institution, hence private by law.

Constantine endowed other churches in Rome, but all, as Krautheimer points out (1983: 23), 'rose on estates which were part of the patrimony that over centuries had accumulated in the hands of the emperor's privy purse, the *res privata*. He further promoted Christianity by authorising the church to receive bequests and by making personal donations. According to the *Liber pontificalis*, an early papal chronology, Constantine gave the papal basilica of St Peter a portfolio of income-generating properties in Syria, Egypt and Mesopotamia (Davis 2000: 18–20).

Thus, by 374, when Ambrose became bishop of Milan, the Christian church had several decades of experience of managing estates and distributing alms. Milan's new bishop came from a family of Roman senior civil servants – Ambrose's father had been prefect of Gaul, Ambrose had been prefect in northern Italy – and so he brought to his appointment the requisite qualifications to frame principles on which to base property rights and welfare practices. Ambrose left a body of writing across a range of genres – tracts, sermons, letters – that depict an author invoking Christian ethics to tilt at pagan conceptions. Ambrose was ambitious, pugnacious and competitive: the title of his treatise *De Officiis* pitted its author against Cicero's *De Officiis*. As much in those sections of Ambrose's *De Officiis* where he agreed with Cicero as in those where he differed, we see a transition from a pagan to a Christian conception of property and welfare.

To summarise Cicero's *De Officiis*, ownership rights did not inhere in property; there were no conceivable grounds for claiming exclusive right of control over anything as long as humanity lived in a state of nature, that is to say, before society had come into being; and only once humanity had come to live together and form society did a right to own property come to be acknowledged. Property rights brought with them a certain tension, because in a society where individuals owned property a dichotomy arose between virtue and expediency. Ambrose made key changes to Cicero's narrative: he substituted paradise for the state of nature but agreed with Cicero that private property was essentially unnatural. Then, he continued:

> God ordained everything to be produced to provide food for everyone in common; his plan was that the earth would be, as it were, the common possession of us all. Nature produced common rights, then; it is greed that has established private rights.[5]

Ambrose was in agreement with Cicero that private property was a social construct. But whereas Cicero derived ownership rights from custom, *vetere occupatione*, and left it at that, Ambrose, by asserting that property rights had their origin in avarice, was put in a position to counsel a remedy for this evil: 'There is such a thing as *benevolentia*, though, and it is closely linked to *liberalitas* ... But *benevolentia* is also separate and distinct from *liberalitas*.'[6] The dichotomy between virtue and expediency that had exercised pagan philosophers was reconciled, then, through *benevolentia*.[7]

---

5  'Sic enim Deus generari iussit omnia ut pastus omnibus communis esset et terra ergo foret omnium quaedam communis poessio. Natura igitur ius commune generavit, usurpatio ius fecit privatum' (Ambrose 2001: 194).

6  'Est autem benevolentia, et coniuncta liberalitati ... Ubi enim deest liberalitas, benevolentia manet' (Ambrose 2001: 215).

7  'Est igitur non solum familiar contubernium honestatis et utilitatis, sed eadem quoque utilitas quae honestas' (Ambrose 2001: 285).

Practical implications followed. One cited by Ambrose was the sale of church valuables to ransom prisoners of war.[8] But there were others. Around this time, churches began building dedicated welfare infrastructures, such as hospitals and almshouses (Burckhardt 1853: 337).

Ambrose was an unbending defender of property rights, in particular of the right of the church to own property, quite logically so because such rights were a prerequisite for dispensing *benevolentia*. Ambrose linked property rights to provision of welfare, and when he took up the cudgels against the emperor Valentinian – the dispute in this case was over the emperor's claim to a particular church in Milan – he inveighed against confiscation because, he asserted, the 'possessions of the church are the maintenance of the poor' (Ambrose 1896: 419). In the circumstances it would have been inconsistent if Ambrose had not impressed this view on his correspondents in his epistolary work: 'But riches themselves are not blameable. For "the ransom of a man's life are his riches," since he that gives to the poor redeems his soul. So that even in these material riches there is a place for virtue' (Ambrose 1896: 470).[9]

A collateral implication of the ethics of property ownership was an appreciation of the intrinsic ethical value of work (Ambrose 1896: 471):

> Reward is not obtained by ease or by sleep. The sleeper does no work, ease brings no profit, but rather loss. Esau

---

8 'Hoc ergo malui vobis liberos tradere quam aurum reservare' (Ambrose 2001: 345).

9 Ambrose here quoted Proverbs 13:8.

by taking his ease lost the blessing of the first-born, for he preferred to have food given to him rather than to seek it. Industrious Jacob found favour with each parent.

## John Chrysostomos in Constantinople

In Rome, the empire's capital of old, Christians were in a minority; in the empire's new capital, Constantinople, Christians were dominant from its very beginning. As Bishop of Constantinople, Chrysostomos enjoyed an incomparably stronger position than Ambrose in Milan and, preaching from the pulpit of the Hagia Sophia, he had the emperor's ear, quite literally, because the emperor was a member of his congregation. Where Ambrose wrote, Chrysostomos spoke: Ambrose, when he drafted his tracts and letters, had in his mind a reader, someone he wished to convince; when Chrysostomos delivered a sermon he had listeners at his feet and aimed to stir them to action. Clearly, he was good at this (Chrysostomos is Greek for 'golden mouthed'). Here, his sermons are relevant because they showed what theological doctrines meant in practice. Specifically, from Chrysostomos's sermons we can extract incipient income demographics, what good a welfare programme would do, and how it could be paid for.

On the demographics of income distribution (John Chrysostomos 1888: 706):

[L]et us inquire, if it seem good, which are more numerous in the city, poor or rich; and which they, who are neither poor nor rich, but have a middle place. As, for instance, a tenth part is of rich, and a tenth of the poor that have nothing at all, and the rest of the middle sort.

On the benefits of a welfare programme (John Chrysostomos 1888: 706):

For the very rich indeed are but few, but those that come next to them are many; again, the poor are much fewer than these ... For if both the wealthy, and those next to them, were to distribute amongst themselves those who are in need of bread and raiment, scarcely would one poor person fall to the share of fifty men or even a hundred ... if ten men only were thus willing to spend, there would be no poor.

On the costs of a welfare programme (John Chrysostomos 1888: 884):

[T]hey that assemble themselves here amount to the number of one hundred thousand; and if each bestowed one loaf to some one of the poor, all would be in plenty; but if one farthing only, no one would be poor.

Sermons such as these had practical implications for welfare provision. Lists of paupers eligible for support were compiled, called *matricula*; according to John Chrysostomos, in Antioch the number came to 3,000 (John Chrysostomos 1888: 706–7).

## Christian versus pagan welfare policies

There remains the question of how we can be sure that the welfare policies of the period would not have crystallised without Christianity; in other words, whether they would have evolved in any event. A testimony by the emperor Julian the Apostate (*c.* 331–63) disposes of this conjecture. We can tell from Julian's appellation that he aimed to restore paganism as the favoured religion of the empire, and thus be considered a witness with an anti-Christian bias. Indeed, Julian revoked many privileges of the church, but he did not shrink from adopting Christian welfare policies for his own purposes. For example, the church historian Sozomen (*c.* 400–*c.* 450) pointed out that the emperor Julian founded 'hospitals for the relief of strangers and of the poor and for other philanthropic purposes' (Sozomen 1855: 228). But Julian was quite conscious that he was thereby adopting Christian practices. In a letter to a certain Arsacius, a pagan high priest, Julian expressly referred to Christianity as the competitive model for welfare policies (Christians are called 'Galileans') (Julian the Apostate 1923: 71):

> I have provided means to meet the necessary expenditure ... to be distributed among strangers and our own poor ... while even the impious Galileans provide not only for those of their own party who are in want, but also for those who hold with us, it would indeed be disgraceful if we were to allow our own people to suffer from poverty.

After Julian died, prematurely, Christianity's grip on the terms of reference for government policy was henceforth unopposed. In 451, the emperor Valentinian III enshrined church welfare policies in law by inserting the following rescript in the *Codex Justinianus*:

> And, for the reason that it becomes Our humanity to provide for those who are poor, and to use Our efforts to prevent indigent persons from wanting food; We order that those things of different kinds which up to this time have been furnished the Holy Churches but of the public property shall remain unaltered, and shall not hereafter be diminished; and We hereby confirm this liberality for all time.[10]

## Patristic economics in the literature

Tertullian, Ambrose and Chrysostomos marked a development that progressed, step by step, from theology to law and to economics. In early Christianity, private property was a prerequisite for the exercise of charitable giving on a voluntary basis; Christian *benevolentia* superseded pagan *liberalitas* as an incentive for welfare. The distribution of welfare on a systematic basis consisted of pragmatic

---

10 'Imperatores Valentinianus, Marcianus: Et quia humanitatis nostrae est prospicere egenis ac dare operam, ut pauperibus alimenta non desint, salaria etiam, quae sacrosanctis ecclesiis in diversis speciebus de publico hactenus ministrata sunt, iubemus nunc quoque inconcussa et a nullo prorsus imminuta praestari liberalitatique huic promptissimae perpetuam tribuimus firmitatem.' Corpus Juris Civilis 1.2.12.2 (http://www.cultura-barocca .com/Imperia/corpus1.htm).

applications of the legal disquisitions of Ambrose complemented by the quantitative feasibility analysis of John Chrysostomos. From ostensibly theological and pastoral works there emerged in Christianity the contours of law and economics.

To return to Schumpeter's and Viner's apodictic assertions, Schumpeter's reading list for the chapter on Church Fathers in his *History of Economic Analysis* includes Tertullian, Ambrose and Chrysostomos, of whom Schumpeter (1954: 71) wrote:

> The opinions on economic subjects that we might find – such as that believers should sell what they have and give it to the poor, or that they should lend without expecting anything (possibly not even repayment) from it – are ideal imperatives that form part of a general scheme of life and express this general scheme and nothing else; least of all scientific propositions.

An explanation may be offered as to how Schumpeter could have advanced his sweeping generalisation without supplying supporting evidence: his magisterial *History of Economic Analysis* was published posthumously and, had he had the opportunity, he might have made revisions to his draft. This presumption is strengthened by considering that Jacob Viner's publication, too, is posthumous; Viner worked on a draft between 1957 and 1962 but had not returned to it before he died in 1970.[11] A final version by

---

11 See the editorial introduction to Viner (1978: 3).

Viner's hand is unlikely to have stated, at least not without further evidence, '[t]here was, as far as I know, no early Christian "wisdom" literature linking individual piety with worldly prudence' (Viner 1978: 12). This assertion is untenable, refuted as it is by innumerable examples; to cite but one, Ambrose's pithy quip, 'money has better use in a poor man's meal than in a rich man's purse'.[12]

Ample literature on welfare policies in early Christianity was to hand, had Schumpeter and Viner only reached for it. Pertinent examples are Johann Uhlhorn's *Christian Charity in the Ancient Church* (1883), and an earlier work that instigated the study of poor relief in early Christianity, Georg Ratzinger's *Geschichte der kirchlichen Armenpflege* (1868), which Ratzinger introduced as the first comprehensive and systematic exploration of the subject of charity in the early church. Ratzinger drew on a wide range of works (many more than are cited in this article) to substantiate his findings; an excerpt from his summary follows (Ratzinger 1868: 110–11):

> The Fathers are tireless in asking to give generous alms, to give often and give much, which is based in part on their strong emphasis on the Christian conception of property. The consistent teaching of the Fathers on property can be summarized in brief as follows. The goods of this world are intended for all humanity in the same way. But according to a wise divine law that humanity should

---

12 '[M]elius operatur pecunia in pauperis cibo quam in divitis sacculo' (Ambrose 2001: 310).

depend on one another, it is impossible for everyone to own at the same time and in the same way: inequality of possessions is rather the express will of God, wherefore there always will be some who are poor and some who are rich, some who have possessions and some who do not. However, possession of something does not imply ownership in the strict sense of the term, but rather that to have been appointed by God as an administrator with a mandate to use only as much as is necessary, applying everything else for the poor.

It seems likely Schumpeter and Viner were unaware of Ratzinger's book, which, however, would have circulated in his wider family. It is pertinent to mention in particular it would have come into the hands of a great-nephew, Joseph Ratzinger, who later became Pope Benedict XVI. I will touch on this connection momentarily, but first I turn to Frank Knight (1939: 420), who asserted,

if we turn to the 'scriptures', the one recognised source of Christian teaching now generally recognised as authoritative, it seems impossible to read into the text any exhortation to, or ideal of, rational efficiency, or progress, in any form. On the contrary, we find quite definite statements that such things do not matter.

Knight might have reached a different conclusion had he engaged with discourse on the nature of property rights instigated by Francis of Assisi and concluded by Pope John XXII.

## Medieval Christian discourse on property rights

Francis was inspired by Jesus' example to renounce material possessions and found a religious order that espoused poverty; John XXII, following a review of scripture, ruled it heretical to claim that Jesus did not have property rights. Before reviewing how Francis and John XXII made use of scriptural evidence in their argumentation, we need to see why property rights mattered so much to Franciscan friars. After Francis died in 1226, a magnificent basilica was built in Assisi. But this testimony to the veneration of Francis presented a visible dilemma: how did this opulent structure fit with renunciation of material wealth in any form? This challenge, how to make the Franciscan ideal of poverty work in practice, grew greater as the Franciscan order expanded and accumulated an estate. Franciscans needed a legal framework for managing an estate without infracting their vow of poverty.

To this complex problem Franciscans offered a simple solution. They invoked two terms from Roman and canon law, *dominium* and *usus*, which corresponded respectively to ownership and use. This dichotomy between owning and using could be grasped intuitively, and Franciscans applied it to the issue before them to argue that in relation to their estate they were users rather than owners. Pope Nicholas III's bull *Exiit qui seminat* of 1279 issued a ruling that seemed practicable.[13] Accordingly, there were four variants of property rights, the first three of which were drawn from

---

13  http://www.papalencyclicals.net/Nichol03/exiit-e.htm

Roman law: *proprietas*, absolute ownership of something; *possessio*, control over something; and *usufructus*, title to enjoying the fruit yielded by something. *Exiit qui seminat* included a fourth term to fit the particular needs of Franciscans, namely *usus simplex facti*, which arose from using an asset but without claiming a right to recurring use in the future. The implication applicable to the Franciscan order was that its members held their endowment by right as users; ownership lay with the Holy See. However, disputes over the property rights of Franciscans did not go away. The literature on this subject grew; what matters for our purpose is that this debate was conducted in legal terms and that references to scripture were scarce. The claim that was central to the Franciscan approach to property, namely that Jesus had been propertyless, was still, a century after Francis had died in 1226, taken for granted.[14]

The accession of John XXII to the papacy heralded a new era in this debate, in two respects: first, through unequivocal endorsement of the right to own property, and, second, through deriving the legitimacy of this right from scripture. John XXII issued four interventions in the debate on property rights, which successively shifted the frame of reference from jurisprudence to scripture. We take these four bulls in turn.

In 1322, the bull *Ad conditorem canonum*[15] disposed of the legal construction Franciscans placed on the capacity

---

14  There is a rich literature on the many facets of this debate which are outside my focus here (see, for example, Lambert 1998).

15  http://individual.utoronto.ca/jwrobinson/translations/john22_acc-com pared.pdf

in which they stood to their fixed and consumable assets, according to which, as already stated, they were users rather than owners. John XXII argued that this claim was intrinsically inconsistent. Regarding fixed assets, *Ad conditorem canonum* pointed out Franciscans had the right to sell their properties, which implied they acted as owners rather than as users ('For who could describe as a "simple usuary" someone permitted to exchange, sell or give away the usuary thing?'). Moreover, Franciscans were usuaries in perpetuity; this was repugnant with the laws on usufruct, since putative owners never regained control of their property and thus were deprived of their *dominium*. Addressing Franciscan use of consumables, *Ad conditorem canonum* argued likewise the terms *usufructus* and *usus simplex facti* did not apply, for it simply made no sense to assert, say, that one could eat an apple without having first taken possession of it. The point of usufruct is to leave the substance of the asset yielding a benefit intact, but in the case of consumables this is impossible. The tone of *Ad conditorem canonum* verges on sarcasm, such as when it poses the rhetorical question 'what sane person' would believe the Lord had wanted his church to retain ownership over 'an egg, or a cheese, or a crust of bread'. When a consumable is used, it is used up.

Predictably, objections were raised to the pope's stance. But two bulls issued in 1324 showed that the stance of the Holy See had hardened. The first, *Quia quorundam*,[16] rebutted claims that Jesus had not owned property, and

---

16 http://www.papalencyclicals.net/John22/qquor-e.htm

asserted the opposite, namely that 'it can be inferred rather that the Gospel life lived by Christ and the Apostles did *not* exclude some possessions in common'. The second, *Cum inter nonnullos*,[17] condemned assertions to the contrary as 'erroneous and heretical'. Now, what had been a jurisprudential contention had become a matter of doctrine. Controversies escalated into acrimony once dissent had become a matter of potential heresy challenging papal authority and competence. Moreover, certain ecclesial and political factions fanned the flames of dissent for reasons of their own (struggles that here are ignored). John XXII returned to the issue of property rights after a five-year gap, in 1329, with the bull *Quia vir reprobus*.[18] A censorious note was already sounded in the introduction: 'Although these attacks are so notoriously unsound as to be not worth answering', he wrote, 'I have thought that brief answer should be made.' In fact, the 'brief' bull is longer than all of his previous three interventions combined.

*Quia vir reprobus* reiterated flaws in the Franciscan distinction between ownership and use: buildings could not qualify as usufruct if they did not revert to an owner; consumables passed into the ownership of a user at the moment of their consumption. Given that a binding conception of property rights could not be derived from law, *Quia vir reprobus* aimed to settle disputes over property rights once and for all by seeking resolution from scripture.

---

17  http://www.franciscan-archive.org/bullarium/qinn-e.html

18  http://www.mq.edu.au/about_us/faculties_and_departments/faculty_of
    _arts/mhpir/staff/staff-politics_and_international_relations/john_kil
    cullen/john_xxii_quia_vir_reprobus/

Before reviewing pertinent references to scripture, let us see what evidence from scripture had been cited by Francis.

The claim that Jesus and his apostles had been propertyless was what underpinned Franciscan attitudes to the legitimacy of private property, and was something that Francis took for granted, it seems. Francis's Rule of 1221 contains only a single citation from scripture concerned with divestment of material goods, namely Jesus' advice to a young man seeking guidance on what he should do to become a follower: 'If thou wilt be perfect, go, and sell what thou hast, and give to the poor, and thou shalt have treasure in heaven; and come, follow me' (Matt. 19: 21; Habig 1983: 31). Since Francis's death in 1226, the assertion that Jesus had been propertyless had stood uncontested. *Quia vir reprobus* of 1329 was the first systematic challenge of the scriptural evidence and propounded that no annulment of property rights could be derived from scripture. Even in the earliest Christianity community, where members 'of one heart and one soul' had sold their possessions and distributed the proceeds, what had taken place was a transfer of ownership from one member to another, which, however, did not revoke the right to own property as such (Acts 2: 44–45 and 4: 32–46). To draw that inference would be fallacious because, since the act of consumption is individual, a consumable cannot become the property of a collective; in other words, anyone who eats an apple owns that apple. *Quia vir reprobus* thus refuted the assertion that the early Christians had rescinded property rights. Moreover, the right to own property was inherent in God's plan for humanity. Already, property rights existed in paradise: Adam was granted *dominium* over the Garden of Eden (Gen. 1: 28). Moreover, property rights continued after Adam and Eve had been expelled from paradise: Abel, Noah and Israel's kings had all owned property. Next, *Quia vir reprobus* demonstrated that Jesus, too, had had rights to property. This was seen when Pilate asked Jesus whether he was king of the Jews, and Jesus declared, 'My kingdom is not from here' (John 18: 36–37). This response made explicit that the kingship of Jesus was divine in origin, and hence contained within its compass all attributes of kingship in the earthly domain; and, as had been seen from the foregoing, kings were entitled to own property. While it was clear from the gospels that Jesus chose not to exercise his ownership right, it would be unwarranted to infer that the right to own property as such was thereby invalidated; a king retained his right to *dominium* even if he resigned himself to a life of poverty.

Proximate to the right to own property was the right to own and use money. *Quia vir reprobus* cited three instances where Jesus and his apostles approved of the use of money. First, Jesus gave an exhortation to lend to anyone in need, which presupposed that a lender was in actual possession of money (Matt. 5: 42). Second, the apostles spent money to buy food for the crowd assembled to hear the Sermon on the Mount (John 4: 8). Third, before the last supper Jesus sent Judas to buy food; the gospel referred explicitly to Judas' purse (John 13: 29).

It remained to be shown whether Jesus' counsel to a young man, 'go and sell everything' and distribute the proceeds to the poor, which had been quoted in Francis's

Rule of 1221, absolved Christians from the need to husband resources and attend to property. *Quia vir reprobus*
cited Jesus' reprimand of a servant who had neglected the
property of his master (Luke 19: 22–24). Jesus made clear
that however great may be the obstacles in the path of a
rich man seeking to pass through the gates of heaven, and
however laudable the inclination of someone who shared
out worldly goods with the poor, a Christian who handles
property is enjoined to apply due care.

John XXII took steps to enshrine his position on
property rights in church practice. In 1317, John XXII
canonised St Louis of Toulouse, whose life was an actual
instance where a scion of a royal dynasty had emulated the example of Jesus. St Louis of Toulouse (1274–97)
was born to the dynasty of Anjou and would have been
a pretender to the throne of Naples, but he preferred to
devote his life to the ministry and lead the life of a simple
Franciscan friar; thus Louis was an apposite example of
John XXII's assertion that kingship was not contingent
on exercising claims to property. In 1323, John XXII canonised St Thomas Aquinas, a prominent advocate of the
right to own property.

*Quia vir reprobus* was a radical break with received conceptions of property rights. Pagans and Christians alike had
considered property a social construct that emerged when
society came into being, but henceforth, now that *Quia
vir reprobus* had projected the origins of property back to
paradise, property rights were considered to be sanctioned
by divine will and to precede rights granted by state and
church. By implication, the right to own property was no

longer in the gift of church or state. Intra-ecclesial altercations with the Franciscan order were not put to an end; specifically, prominent Franciscan disputants, such as William of Ockham and Marsilius of Padua, elaborated a conception of property rights independent of state authority. But John XXII made a lasting impact by emancipating the right to property from church and state authority and thus paved the way for a new economic treatment of property. One example may be adduced. John Locke in his *Second Treatise on Government* (1689) elaborated a theory of property rights that had a far-reaching impact on the philosophy of natural rights. Arguably, he developed his theory independently; however, his library contained the literature discussed here, and as Janet Coleman has pointed out, 'it clearly would not have been wise for the politically astute Whig Locke to cite a Catholic and scholastic in support of his own ideas on property' (Coleman 1985: 98).

## Summary

There were two distinct stages in the evolution of the economics of property rights in early and medieval Christianity. The first phase covered a period of imperial legal reforms that conduced to the institutionalisation of Christianity and concluded when John Chrysostomos demonstrated that welfare provision was not only a moral imperative but a feasible policy option. By underpinning his claim with a quantification of costs and benefits, John Chrysostomos introduced into Christianity economics based on quantitative evidence.

The second phase began when Francis of Assisi questioned whether the right to own property was compatible with Christianity. But, however radical his challenge in substance, Francis had adduced a single quotation from scripture in his Franciscan Rule, whereas Pope John XXII derived a definitive stance on the right to own property from a review of scriptural evidence that was comprehensive and systematic. John XXII achieved a twofold result: from then on, the legitimacy of owning property was argued on its merits, and by implication the right to own property was no longer contingent on legitimisation by ecclesial or secular authority. The ramifications of these innovations are wider than the dimensions of this article.[19] Several centuries of medieval discourse preceded the framework of property rights that are commonly credited to the Enlightenment, a process triggered by probing questions regarding the ethics of property ownership posed by Francis of Assisi.

Three authoritative economists of the twentieth century were cited in this article. The point of doing so was not thereby to show that the economics of the first phase had been overlooked by Joseph Schumpeter and Jacob Viner, or that Frank Knight was wrong about the progressive content of the second. The point of this juxtaposition was to accentuate the perspective on medieval economics elucidated by Georg Ratzinger (who as far as I can tell is here quoted in anglophone literature for the first time)

---

19 Michael Allen Gillespie (2008) and Ismail Kurun (2016), for example, have argued that the discourse of Pope John XXII marked an incipient trajectory that in due course unfolded the rationality of the Enlightenment.

that portended the encyclical *Caritas in Veritate* of Pope Benedict XVI of 2009, which issued pronouncements on the ethics of property rights and of welfare.[20] To see that the economics of property rights of the present links back to the second century may reward a reader tracing this trajectory with a sense of surprise.

---

20 http://w2.vatican.va/content/benedict-xvi/en/encyclicals/documents/hf _ben-xvi_enc_20090629_caritas-in-veritate.html

# 6 SIR THOMAS MORE'S *UTOPIA*: AN OVERLOOKED ECONOMIC CLASSIC

Esa Mangeloja and Tomi Ovaska

Sir Thomas More's book *Utopia* from 1516 is seen as a basic founding text for the theoretical corpus of modern political science. Still a popular figure in modern British literary history, More was placed at number 37 in the BBC's poll of the 100 Greatest Britons in 2002 (Parrill and Robison 2013: 92). We argue that *Utopia* is significant as a political text, but perhaps even more so as an economic text. In fact, *Utopia* has enough modern economics to be used as an educational text in subjects such as economic development, comparative economic systems and history of economic thought or even principles of economics. Then again, the demise of common property-based socialism around 1990 decreased both popular and academic interest in More's *Utopia*, as Marxism–Leninism faded.

Seeing common property as the sole significant concept in *Utopia*, however, is somewhat defective and specious. Instead, we argue that certain additional important themes, such as religion, should not be downgraded in the analysis. The idea of common property has been present as one valid alternative in Christian thinking from the beginning of the Church. A communal way of life existed in the early Christian congregation in Jerusalem during the times of New Testament, but its expansion to other areas was fairly limited. There clearly existed a communal way of life after the death of Christ in Jerusalem, but the expansion of the use of common property diminished when the central geographical core of early Christianity was transposed from Jerusalem to Antioch. After an extended break, however, Thomas More used the concept of common property once again in its religious context.

Schwartz (1989) comments on More's apparent religious leanings in the book. *Utopia* has a unique theological utopia at its philosophical core, which is intertwined with its economic concepts, common property in particular. In *Utopia*, the worldview is clearly Christian in nature, as most citizens in *Utopia* are devout Christians. It is also clearly stated that a man who refuses to believe in God or the afterlife could never be trusted, because he would not be able to acknowledge any authority or principle outside himself. This statement will turn out to be of great importance when discussing *Utopia*'s potential as a viable economic system.

*Utopia* is regularly discussed in a wide swathe of academic fields. These include history, philosophy, political science, religion and sociology, to name a few. Depending on the writer, *Utopia* has been viewed as a defence of individual freedom, a showcase of a conflict between the medieval and the modern worlds, a critique of the European society of its time, a blueprint for socialism, a display of a path to a moral, virtuous life, an astute analysis of society's social structures, or a portrayal of the minimum conditions for a happy life (Ackroyd 1999; Marius 1984). Another common interpretation over the years has been that through *Utopia* More wanted to highlight the benefits of common property in maintaining a happy citizenry. Since the collapse of the socialist system, this line of thinking has lost most of its vigour, though.

Some scholars have interpreted *Utopia* in much less progressive terms, arguing that More wrote it as nothing more than a parody, aiming to expose the impossibility of organising societies around common property; thus, More's book is filled with the rhetorical devices of irony and wit. Bostaph (2006) also suggests that various internal contradictions in *Utopia* only strengthen the view that *Utopia* is really a satire and that More was well aware of the indispensability of money in complex societies. Wood (1999) for his part considers *Utopia* to be more like a comic illustration than an ideal, functioning society. In his view *Utopia* is a darkly ironic vision of a state made possible only by luck and divine interference. The lives of the Utopians are portrayed as dour and grim, the natural result of a planned society.

According to several other scholars, *Utopia* was not intended as a jest. Karl Kautsky (1888: 247) wrote:

> The idea that it was written as a jest may be dismissed. It was taken very seriously by More's contemporaries. Budaeus, for example, wrote to Lupsetus: 'We are greatly indebted to Thomas More for his Utopia, in which he holds up to the world a model of social felicity. Our age

and our posterity will regard this exposition as a source
of excellent doctrines and useful ordinances, from which
States will construct their institutions.'

Numerous other contemporaries of More express themselves in a similar way. These include scholars and statesmen like Johannes Paludanus, Paulus Jonius and Hierony-
mus Buslidianus.

Some concepts in *Utopia* have had a striking staying
power over centuries. It is known now that common property did not work in reality in the socialist economies.[1] But
More's system was built differently, drawing its strength
from theocratic order. In his view only heavenly law, established and monitored by divine autarchy and absolute
authority, would enable the working of common property
in society. This insight is key to opening *Utopia* to a new
economic–institutional interpretation. *Utopia*'s strong religious ideas are inseparably tied to economics and its economic system. Religion gives people incentives that society's other institutions require if they are to work properly.

This chapter next analyses the theological core of *Utopia*,
namely common property, and describes daily life in *Utopia*.
Then, a section highlights the wealth and fine detail of economic concepts at the heart of *Utopia*. This is followed by
a discussion of economic systems, aiming to place *Utopia*
within the traditional systems classification. Since every
economic system, save pure anarchy, depends on a set of

---

1   Presumably because he advocated common property, More is the only
    Christian saint honoured with a statue at the Kremlin.

rules to work properly, ways to enforce rules are then discussed. This is followed by an evaluation of the expected outcomes from different economic systems. The final, key question addressed in this chapter is whether *Utopia* would actually work in real life: would it be viable in the sense that it would satisfy the needs of its citizens in perpetuity?

## The theological core of *Utopia*: common property

More joins a long succession of Christian utopians who have used ancient biblical material for constructing a futuristic vision of the coming messianic theocracy, as foreseen in *Utopia*.[2] More's ideology was apparently Christian, as most citizens of Utopia were devout Christians. For example, 'true it is, that many of them came over to our religion, and were initiated into it by baptism' (p. 118). People living in Utopia had complete freedom of faith, even though most citizens were actually Christians. Other religions were equally accepted; only the atheists were clearly despised. As More put it (p. 118):

> [H]e therefore left men wholly to their liberty, that they
> might be free to believe as they should see cause; only
> he made a solemn and severe law against such as should
> so far degenerate from the dignity of human nature, as

---

2   After More, several other Christian utopias appeared during the sixteenth and seventeenth centuries. Those include *Wolfaria* (1521) by Johan Eberlin Von Günzburg (1470–1533) and *Christianopolis* (1619) by Johann Valentin Andreae (1586–1654). The properties of these various utopias are presented in detail by Davis (1981) and Bell (1967).

to think that our souls died with our bodies, or that the world was governed by chance, without a wise overruling Providence: for they all formerly believed that there was a state of rewards and punishments to the good and bad after this life; and they now look on those that think otherwise as scarce fit to be counted men, since they degrade so noble a being as the soul, and reckon it no better than a beast's: thus they are far from looking on such men as fit for human society, or to be citizens of a well-ordered commonwealth; since a man of such principles must needs, as oft as he dares do it, despise all their laws and customs: for there is no doubt to be made, that a man who is afraid of nothing but the law, and apprehends nothing after death, will not scruple to break through all the laws of his country, either by fraud or force, when by this means he may satisfy his appetites. They never raise any that hold these maxims, either to honours or offices, nor employ them in any public trust, but despise them, as men of base and sordid minds.

As Kanter (1972: 136–38) notes, strong religious foundations have the ability to tie communities together, even when combined with an ideology of common property. A common religion gives communities a comprehensive value system, a transcendent moral order with many advantageous moral principles, and a web of shared beliefs.

More was a man of many faces. He valued structure, tradition and order in society as safeguards against tyranny and error. While More promoted education in *Utopia*, some years later, in 1528, he warned that the English Bible must not get into the wrong hands. According to him, it was especially dangerous when unlearned men look for and dispute the secret mysteries of the Bible. More also strongly opposed Martin Luther and the Protestant Reformation, judging them to be dangerous for the stability of society. Paradoxically, More prescribed freedom of religion in *Utopia*, except for atheists, who were despised, and only just tolerated. More himself persecuted Protestants during his time as the Lord Chancellor and fought against the rising Reformation. While Lord Chancellor, he also imprisoned and interrogated Lutherans, and sent six reformers to be burned at the stake, in addition to imprisoning about forty Protestants. Ackroyd (1999) adopts a rather understanding perspective on these acts; according to him, they were part of a long-standing Protestant and Catholic tradition in turbulent religious times. Indeed, in section 4 of his Apostolic Letter of 31 October 2000, declaring More 'The Heavenly Patron of Statesmen and Politicians', Pope John Paul II observed:

> It can be said that he demonstrated in a singular way the value of a moral conscience ... even if, in his actions against heretics, he reflected the limits of the culture of his time.

Biblical materials provide the basis for More's penchant for common property. Two distinct versions of theocratic utopia can actually be found in the New Testament. One is found in Acts, which depicts the social life of the first years of the Church in Jerusalem, soon after Christ's resurrection and ascension and after the first Pentecost. Among the first Christians, there seems to have been common property, similar to the ideology found in *Utopia*. Acts 4: 32 says:

> And the multitude of them that believed were of one heart and of one soul: neither said any of them that ought of the things which he possessed was his own; but they had all things common.

Nevertheless, this original state of the early Church in Jerusalem was temporary, and the convention of common property did not spread widely to other early congregations or synagogues. Nevertheless, More seems to have adopted this idea from the writings of the New Testament. Utopian visions were also common during the days of the Hebrew Bible.

Biblical eschatology has been an important part of both Judaism and Christianity. Those visions included economic aspects. Jewish history describes periods of captivity of the Jewish people in Egypt and Babylon in different periods. That certainly contributed to the development of the idea of a utopia. The captivity was ended by the only true God, an act which stood in stark contrast to the idolatry of the multitude of gods worshipped in Egypt and Babylon. Christian apocalyptic writings (such as Revelation) are inspired by Jewish eschatology, and also appear in a context of difficulties for the early Christians. The practice of common property vanished as the epicentre of early Christianity moved from Jerusalem to Asia Minor.

Perhaps the theological core of More's *Utopia* is partly derived from another part of the Bible, not from past temporary situations among the early Christians, but from the future messianic kingdom ideology. This political theocratic utopia is found in many books of the Bible, both in the Hebrew Bible and the New Testament. This is the very ideology Jesus was preaching: the coming of 'the kingdom of heaven' on earth, among the human race. The ideology of the coming kingdom of heaven is found, for example, in the book of Revelation (20: 1–6):

> Then I saw an angel coming down from heaven, having the key to the bottomless pit and a great chain in his hand. He laid hold of the dragon, that serpent of old, who is the Devil and Satan, and bound him for a thousand years ... so that he should deceive the nations no more till the thousand years were finished ... Then I saw the souls of those who had been beheaded for their witness to Jesus and for the word of God, who had not worshipped the beast or his image, and had not received his mark on their foreheads or on their hands. And they lived and reigned with Christ for a thousand years ... Over such the second death has no power, but they shall be priests of God and of Christ, and shall reign with Him a thousand years.

Intertwining theology and theocratic governance with scarcity of natural resources was not a problem for More. He forecast in *Utopia* that hardships would be overcome by God's help (p. 107):

> They are also persuaded that God will make up the loss
> of those small pleasures with a vast and endless joy, of
> which religion easily convinces a good soul.

More's original audience consisted of the priests and theologians of his time, not the educated classes generally. It should be remembered that it was a well-known and established theologian, Erasmus of Rotterdam, who actually published *Utopia* in 1516. One additional piece of evidence for this claim is that *Utopia* was published only in Latin. It was translated into English and published in England long after More's execution for high treason in 1535, and not earlier than 1551, over fifteen years after his death. This suggests that More's intention was theological and philosophical. As Kautsky (1888) notes, More addressed only a small circle of scholars; most people did not understand him and he did not want them to. He therefore wrote *Utopia* in Latin, and concealed his thoughts in the guise of satire, which permitted him greater freedom of opinion. He was almost certainly not aiming to affect the politics of his time.

*Utopia* can also be seen as defending religious tolerance. Kessler (2002: 207) suggests that More's aim was to promote civic peace in society and religious freedom for Christians. He enabled government to proscribe politically dangerous forms of religion, and all members of society to subscribe to certain Christian religious doctrines that promoted virtue. This restricted type of religious freedom made Utopia a theologically diverse but morally unified society.

More promoted social and political equality. The economic reforms More advocated include common ownership of property, the abolition of profit and the obligation and right of all to labour. He tried to establish social equality by protecting the rights of good conscience. *Utopia* contains several institutional devices to bring about social equality, like common meals, a common form of clothing, and homes that were open to all. The false sense of superiority that fosters idleness and luxury among the wealthy and leads them to exploit the poor was removed from the lives of Utopian people (Kessler 2002: 219).

It should also be noted that the conduct of the Utopians is exaggerated even by Christian standards. While the utopian way of life embodies certain truths dear to Christianity, it frequently exceeds Christian tolerance. It is as though without the correcting guidance of Christ's Church the Utopians would fall into absurdity (Grace 1989: 293).

Jackson (2000) notes that More resembled Machiavelli in his aim to create a peaceful political order. To attain that, even a degree of immorality in political conduct was justified. *Utopia* works through paradox and indirect persuasion to restore truly Christian judgement in political life. More's strategy was not simply to reassert what was familiar to everybody, namely that Christian precepts ought to be followed, but rather that uncontrolled appetites were the basis of social vices. This implies that a fallen nature needed the discipline of external restraints if there was to be peace and justice. Therefore, More adopted a utopian view of an optimal economic and political order, using religious concepts and themes (Grace 1989: 295).

## Economic concepts in *Utopia*

*Utopia* is replete with economic concepts, many of which had no name at the time of More's writing but which are nowadays widely recognised. One of the standard concepts in economics is scarcity; there are only so many resources to supply people's unlimited wants. In this respect, Utopians were model citizens. Their consumption of goods and services was limited to necessities, and through science, specialisation and experimentation they had reached quite a high level of efficiency in meeting their needs. Economising was apparent everywhere, the prevailing philosophy stressing that one did not need more than basic goods and nourishment for a pleasurable life, a view which is consistent with many current studies of life satisfaction. The Utopians showed an understanding of the marginal product of labour. They limited their working day to a mere six hours. They also used scarcity to create exchange value. For *Utopia* itself the intrinsic value of gold and silver was set at zero, although large amounts of both were mined. Since the exchange value was very high outside its borders, *Utopia*'s inhabitants sold their minerals through mutually beneficial transactions (arbitrage) in the foreign trade market.

Hanging of thieves in societies outside Utopia is an example of the use of cost–benefit analysis. For a thief outside Utopia the choice was to starve to death or to steal with a reasonable chance of getting away with it. Not surprisingly, the death penalty was not effective in stopping thefts. On the Utopian side the same calculation was different. Being caught thieving would result in hard labour and the disapproval of the community, but not death. Every citizen of Utopia was guaranteed the same ration of food and other goods, and accumulation of private property was forbidden. Not surprisingly, there was less theft within Utopia than outside it. In an example of the kind of cost–benefit analysis practiced in Utopia, a wealthy prince took a nearby kingdom by force. The result was a years-long string of internal rebellions and foreign invasions in the newly acquired dominion. The finances of both kingdoms were soon in deficit and the citizenry upset over their meaninglessly spilt blood. In the end, the costs and benefits of the invasion were so uneven that the invader gave up the new dominion. Interestingly, Utopia also spent resources on wars, but only to stay away from them.

Large sections of *Utopia* are about good governance and the importance of institutions. Thorstein Veblen (1912) was a forerunner of modern institutionalism, preceding by three generations later neo-institutionalist writers such as Bauer (1971), Olson (1982) and North (1990). The way Veblen merged institutions and cultural/spiritual attitudes makes for a striking resemblance to Utopia's way of life. Utopia without spiritual underpinnings simply couldn't exist. Veblen also emphasised the role of evolutionary thinking. Unlike with communism, there was no particular end to the development of societies, an idea which meshes well with the educational and spiritual aspirations of *Utopia*. Given the limited variety of goods and services produced in Utopia, it is also clear that even if the society was productively efficient, it was far removed from Veblen's conspicuous consumption, and also certainly lacking allocative efficiency in production. Then again, since Utopians had no comparison point for a 'sufficient' variety of goods and services, this may not have reduced their ultimate life satisfaction.

Institutions and governance are important concepts in *Utopia*. From the first pages, it is explained how not to govern, with princes ignoring their own countries and focusing on acquiring new possessions through wars. Efficient laws outside Utopia were allegedly rare, the laws being incoherent and punishments in no proportion to crimes. Judicial independence was non-existent; judges were not concerned about making inconsistent decisions. For Utopia the lesson was that when the moral decay begins it spreads quickly, surrounding people with ill company and corruption. That is the beginning of the end for the rule of law.

In Utopia, there was relatively little judicial regulation (fewer laws, more reliance on people's religious virtue). Legal consistency was achieved throughout the island, the same laws applying in all cities. It was a widely accepted idea that strict obedience of the law brings virtuous men joy and keeps society healthy. Utopia's court structure had similarities to that of the modern day. The Governor (head of the larger family group) was like a mediator, the Magister the lower court, the Senate the appeals court, and the Prince, on the rarest of occasions, the Supreme Court. The system did not, however, incorporate the separation of powers as understood nowadays. The executive – the Prince in particular – enjoyed much greater powers than those of modern democratic legislatures and judiciaries.

Some other government functions in Utopia also share many similarities with those in modern societies. A common theme in the text is how education is greatly under-appreciated (a public good with positive externalities, under-provided by markets) outside Utopia, where, in contrast, it was seen as enhancing the production process and therefore productivity. Hence, government approached public-goods market failure by taking responsibility for education.

A well-acknowledged method of productive improvement in Utopia was trial and error, still used in modern societies by innovative firms and governments alike. The widely used trial-and-error method bore more resemblance to Schumpeterian entrepreneurs (without the personal profit motive and private property rights to innovation) than to the extreme error avoidance of socialist systems (plan is law). Increasing production quantities, however, was not the goal of the government. Rather, productivity increases were meant to allow the production of the same amount of (better) goods in less time. This released extra time to people for intellectual development. The above is a classic case of the trade-offs every economy faces: here the choice was more goods and the same leisure time, or more leisure time and the same amount of goods. As with every trade, there is no avoiding the opportunity cost – if you want more goods there will be less leisure time, and vice versa. The existence of common property also allowed for seamless, quick exchange and operationalisation of innovations among economic units.

The Utopian government did exercise strict population control. It had estimated an upper limit of the population the island could support, and reaching the limit triggered the creation of new colonies on the nearby mainland. A constant theme of discussion in Utopia was the misuse of government power. One neighbouring country, Macaria, was discussed as a virtuous example of how to limit the power of government, keeping it from turning bad: the people had placed a constitutional limit on the spending power of their government. The limit was large enough to allow occasional budget surpluses to flow to a rainy-day fund against unforeseen events. The purported utility maximisation rule of most foreign governments was seen as utterly deceptive, consisting mostly of revenue maximisation for the benefit of the ruling class, and not creating useful societal habits.

Income distribution in Utopia was set to achieve strict equality, which was considered to provide positive externalities. This was the result of Utopians' religious beliefs and also of the excess vanity and consumption disparity that they believed led to moral decay, just as Veblen (1912) also postulated 400 years later with his concept of conspicuous consumption. In Utopia employment security was guaranteed for everyone (as in the Soviet constitution), since unemployment was considered dangerous for the health of the human spirit. As long as a worker did his share, he stayed within the employment-bound social safety net. The length of the working day was set by government regulation at six hours, after which the rest of the day was to be used for intellectually inspiring activities in arts and education. To avoid boredom at work, regulations called for periodic job circulation. A select few Utopians were exempted from regular work, allowing them to specialise in the areas of their exceptional talents (much like in the Soviet Union), aimed at producing scientific discoveries.

Since agricultural yield varies from year to year and from city to city, the Utopian government redistributed the output equally among the cities once a year (progressive taxation), while also preserving a constant two-year reserve of grain. The strong religious ethic of the people would ensure that even a high taxation rate would not result in a productive disincentive. Government had built social safety nets for regular citizens. Utopia's public hospitals, yet another service with public good and externality properties, were also described as excellent.

The Utopians considered the alleged connection between wealth and happiness to be spurious. Wealth by itself was considered not worth pursuing, except where poverty and income inequality existed. Poverty created unwarranted obedience towards those with financial means, while it also negatively affected public safety and social stability. According to Utopians, true happiness was based on following natural reason and religion. Living with reverence to God and nature, and demonstrating true altruism that advances the welfare of the rest of the mankind, were seen as the only ways to true happiness. In discussing the natural way of life and morality, Hodgson (2013) refers to Darwin's evolutionary theory; humans are by their nature prone to reciprocity, cooperation and kindness to each other because that has proved to be a successful trait in human evolution. Sustaining and strengthening this genetic trait was considered one of the government's main goals in Utopia.

Rulers outside Utopia were described as vain and un-interested in good advice. In other words, the rulers were showing the classic signs of overconfidence bias. Their ideal world was one where things would never change and they would be assured of their possessions for ever: the status quo effect was dominating their minds. Rulers pouring resources year after year into defending a new dominion, without any hope of permanent victory, is nothing but a typical example of the sunk-cost fallacy. In fact, examples of other behavioural economics concepts abound in Utopia at regular intervals. These include anchoring, endowment effect, confirmation bias, herd mentality, hyperbolic discounting bias, loss aversion and mental accounting.

## The fundamental goal of all economic systems

Every working economic system has to be able to answer three questions: what to produce, how to produce it, and who gets what is produced. *Utopia*'s answer to the first question is heavily focused on satisfying society's basic needs: food, clothing and shelter. In addition, a number of resources are extended to education, science, health and national defence. The exact distribution of resources to each area is not disclosed. It is noted, though, that health and education are at a good level, science is world class, and the permanent budget for hiring foreign armies for Utopia's defence is sufficient without doubt.

How output is produced in Utopia follows tried and tested methods, namely specialisation and trial and error. Improvements to production techniques are derived particularly from investments in science and education and the shared knowledge base among production units. Utopia also has a policy to match individuals' special skills with their talents, and to allow those with extraordinary talents to dedicate their lives to scientific discovery.[3] These answers to questions one and two – what and how to produce – mean that Utopia's productivity growth comes out high enough to create a production surplus in most years. This it can use to create an emergency surplus, or to reduce daily work time, which in turn allows more time for individual after-work self-improvement.

The answer to question three – how the output is distributed – follows three basic principles. First, equality in sharing is the overriding principle of all distribution. The poorest are taken care of first, as are those families whose harvest yield has fallen below that of the others. Second,

3   This is the same concept of specialisation that Adam Smith popularised more than two centuries later. *Utopia* deserves to be compared to a magnum opus like the *Wealth of Nations* because of three particularly interesting properties. First, the book covers all the basic economics concepts that one would typically find in the first chapter of a modern economics textbook. Second, More succeeded in introducing these basic concepts in 160 highly entertaining and intellectually stimulating pages, mixing economics with politics, religion and evolutionary theory. Third, the book preceded the *Wealth of Nations* by 260 years.

This is by no means meant to imply that More matched the numerous economic insights put forth by Smith. Indisputably, though, *Utopia* was well ahead of its time, and because of its economic depth could well accompany any introductory, or even more advanced, economics textbook as supplemental reading on the choices in society building.

given that yields in agriculture vary considerably from year to year, enough production was always stored for an extra two years' needs in case of a crisis. Third, some surplus is sent abroad, as inexpensive loans, as foreign aid or as finance for foreign armies for Utopia's defence. This serves the country's altruistic goals, creates political goodwill and ensures credible military defence when needed.

## Defining and enforcing the rules of economic systems

An economic system is a set of institutional arrangements used to allocate society's scarce resources to their best purposes, the meaning of 'best' varying over time and by society. The best could include, for instance, longevity, high income, equal distribution of income, opportunities to advance in life, minimal use of environmental resources, religious freedom or overall happiness.

Scarcity means that societies will always be constrained by their lack of land, labour, capital and entrepreneurial skills. Institutional set-up governs how society deals with this scarcity. This set-up is a mix of formal and informal arrangements that include elements such as the parliament and its voting traditions, government agencies and ministries, the Church, the rule of law, the monetary system, trade unions, freedom to trade, civil groups, corporations, international organisations, and suchlike. For an economic system to work the institutions have to follow what North (1990) calls the 'rules of the game'. Without an agreement on the rules, no system will be functional for long. Furthermore, to build an enduring economic system there has to be a means of enforcing the set of rules. If institutions have a proclivity to deviate from the rules with impunity, it's akin to having no rules at all. An important question is: how to ensure adherence to the rules? Religion, altruism and common property represented some of More's answers to the question.

More's answers are in line with modern economic research applying social norms and several categories of informal mechanisms. One such main category, which is in use in Utopia, is community enforcement. Citizens change their trading partners periodically. This exposes dishonest traders, should there be any, causing immediate sanctions against them by other members of the society. Kandori (1992) has presented an economic model, the 'Folk Theorem', where similar social norms to those found in *Utopia* work to support efficient outcomes in various economic transactions. In small communities, where members can observe each other's behaviour, community enforcement works beneficially towards optimal economic outcomes, and cooperative behaviour can be sustained. The social norm supporting cooperation in those situations means that defection from honesty bears a very high cost – potential isolation. As Kandori (1992) notes, the Folk Theorem assumes the existence of a mechanism or institution whose function, as in Utopia, is to process information honestly.

In Table 1, Voigt and Engerer (2002) present a set of five options for rule enforcement. The continuum of the type of rules runs from convention to government legislation, and that of the enforcement types from self-enforcement to organised government enforcement. Modern societies use all five means of enforcement, although in different proportions. Many Western high-income countries have been slowly moving towards more state enforcement, whereas many fast-growing lower-income countries have less state enforcement and some are consciously deregulating their economies. In the group of low-income countries one typically finds much less state enforcement and more of the first four types of rule enforcement: self-enforcing, self-commitment, informal social control and organised private enforcement.

**Table 1    Types of rule and means of enforcement**

| Type of rule | Means of enforcement |
| --- | --- |
| 1. Convention | Self-enforcement |
| 2. Ethical rule | Self-commitment |
| 3. Customs | Informal social control |
| 4. Private rule | Organised private enforcement |
| 5. State law | Organised state enforcement |

*Source*: Voigt and Engerer (2002: 133).

In terms of rule enforcement, More clearly distanced himself from the one system – the English one – that he knew best. Rather than relying on state enforcement, he envisioned that any society viable over the long term would have to be based on other means of enforcement. While there was also strong state law in Utopia, most of the means of enforcement were left to the first four means of enforcement. The convention rule worked because Utopia was not a fast-changing society. The ethical rule worked because everyone in Utopia shared strong religious beliefs about right and wrong. Customs and private rule worked because the tight-knit family would exert social pressure on any member who deviated from the customs. While the state of Utopia had many explicit rules of conduct, rarely did it have to enforce its rules: the four non-state means worked well enough. This is in line with the findings of Frank (1987), who emphasises that conscience and other moral sentiments play a powerful role in the choices people make.

While all economies are unique, one can still try to place them in a loose structure of attributes. In Table 2, system 3 resembles socialism and central planning as practised in the former Soviet Union until 1990. System 2 is an example of market socialism, and had its closest match in the former Yugoslavia in the 1970s and 1980s. System 1 has the characteristics of a pure capitalist free market system. For that system there are no closely fitting examples. Various market failures associated with that system have called for governments much larger in size and wider-reaching in their scope than the pure system would encompass. The reasons for this deviation include market failures in the areas of information, property rights, externalities, public goods and competition. Of current economies, the countries closest to system (1) would probably be Hong Kong, Singapore and New Zealand (Gwartney et al. 2018). When compared with these three system types, Utopia's system is unconventional, drawing its strength from an eclectic mix of attributes. (An augmented table of system classification appears in Figure 1.)

**Table 2    Attributes of economic systems**

| Attribute | Continua | | |
|---|---|---|---|
| A Organisation of decision-making | Decentralisation | Split between levels | Centralisation |
| B Provision of information and coordination | Market | Planned market | Plan |
| C Property rights/ ownership of assets | Private | Cooperative | Public |
| D Incentive system/ motivational method | Material | Moral and material | Moral |
| O Organisation of public choices | Democracy | Oligarchy | Dictatorship |
| Type of system | 1 Free market | 2 Market socialism | 3 Socialism |

*Source*: Adapted from Gregory and Stuart (2004: 30).

Economic systems are built to achieve desired outcomes, which vary from society to society. The choice of an economic system, however, is a good predictor of the expected outcomes. Typically, system 3 in Table 2 would reduce income disparity and strengthen society's social capital, while having low-income growth. System 1 has its strength in income growth and efficiency, but can cause large income disparities. The middle system, system 2, would be expected to yield outcomes similar to system 3. Since neither system 3 nor system 2 survived more than seventy years, system 1, or rather its mixed cousins, has proved to be capable of adjusting to changing circumstances in its environments, enhancing its chances of remaining viable for the long run. It is clear, however, that Table 2 lacks one dimension essential for all economic activity in Utopia: religion and habits. While the economic core of Utopia is built on the combination of common property, religion and habits, it does also have market-based institutions that keep it from being a pure planned economy.

It is commonly argued that the Soviet experience proved Marx, Engels and Lenin wrong about man's real nature: in the real world people are self-interested beings whose basic nature cannot be changed even with the best of educational efforts. That is allegedly why common property did not succeed in the Soviet Union and won't succeed anywhere else either.

Fehr and Gächter (2000) argue that the above reasoning is wrong. While people can be highly self-interested, they can also show astoundingly high levels of kindness when they themselves have just been subjected to a kind act. People feel obliged to treat others in the way others treat them. Such reciprocity is one of the keys to understanding Utopia. Religion was at the centre of all activities in Utopia and, regardless of the type of religion practiced, Utopians emphasised the importance of treating other people kindly. Thus, the reciprocity principle of kindness had a strong foothold in Utopia. In conventional socialist systems there was no such reinforcing mechanism coming from religion and virtuous habits.

Utopia also had another key advantage over common property–based socialist systems. Utopia's basic economic units, namely families, were small in size and all members lived together. Each family had about forty adults, which, as Ostrom (1998) notes, makes setting social norms easier and more binding. Equally important, as Barclay (2011) points out, it is easier to be altruistic to one's kin than to strangers, which further strengthens the reciprocity principle within Utopia's family structure. Altruism has additional benefits: stronger social connections, improved health, chances for cooperative learning, a better emotional life and greater general happiness (Batson 2011).

Figure 1 expands on Table 2, adding a new dimension, namely religion, to the basic system classification. Whereas Table 2 was about systems in theory, in Figure 1 real economic systems are evaluated. The real-life capitalist/market-based system is easily distinguishable from the socialist/central planning-based system. Utopia, on the other hand, included features of both systems. In terms of property rights, socialism and Utopia are alike. They also both include their moral incentives, which, however, turned out to be ineffective under socialism. In Utopia, on the other hand, all institutions were distinctly designed to promote altruism and cooperation, making them the backbone of society.

All modern capitalist systems are mixed, with a relatively large government presence. In most such systems people are free to put their ideas into practice as long as they stay within the regulations and laws, whose extent varies from country to country. In Utopia there was much less freedom in this respect. Although people were encouraged to study and experiment with new ideas in production and within their family unit, their lives were highly structured outside the study time that followed the six-hour working day. While decision-making in capitalism is more decentralised than in Utopia, it is also true that in the average wealthy country government is by no means small: it spends about 40 per cent of the national income on buying goods and services and on income redistribution, in addition to administering thousands of regulations that govern its citizens' lives.

Figure 1    Utopia in a systems map

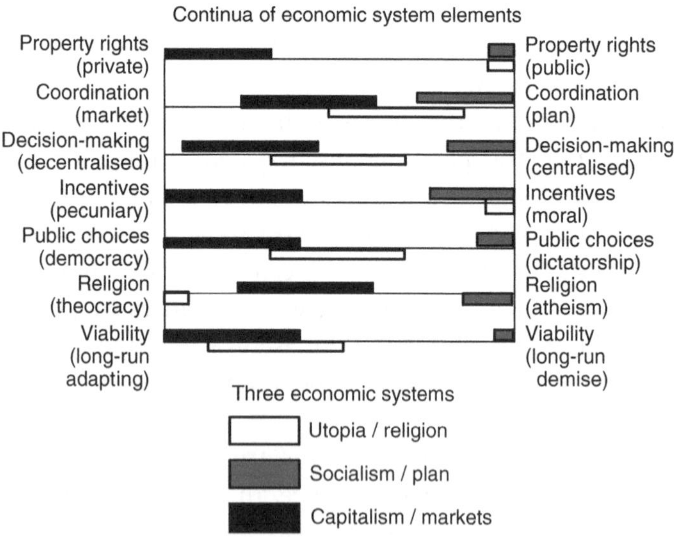

Source: Adapted from Gregory and Stuart (2004: 31).

While hard to estimate, the Utopian government was considerably smaller than governments in typical mixed economies – less government was needed because of Utopia's internal governing system (religious beliefs, habits). Other than very limited public works (select government transfers, the justice system, hospitals, science, temples, transportation, warfare) most economic activity was concentrated in the forty-member families. The system attribute of religion most distinguishes Utopia from socialism and capitalism. Utopia was a pure theocracy, whereas atheism was the rule in socialist countries, and capitalism falls somewhere between the two – in most countries closer to Utopia than to socialism.

Finally, the ultimate question about any economic system is whether it is viable. Will it be able to satisfy the needs of its people in the long run? What we know about socialism is that no version of it has been able to survive for more than seventy years, market socialism even less. Capitalism, on the other hand, has been in existence since the Industrial Revolution, for around 250 years. During this time it has faced several life-threatening crises (excess output volatility, income inequality, and so on) yet so far it has always been able to adjust and to continue in an amended form. The crises will no doubt keep coming, and it remains to be seen whether capitalism will have the ability to continue adjusting to unforeseen future crises. Having already survived for ten generations, though, capitalism has shown a good deal of resilience. Utopia is harder to evaluate. Religion was the glue that held its common property-based system together. The system also required the strict rule-based structure for people's daily lives to stay in place. If those arrangements hold, Utopia should be viable as a system, unlike the other common property–based system, namely socialism.

## Even if an economic system works, does it fulfil people's needs?

An economic system may answer satisfactorily the three basic questions of what, how and for whom, but that does not mean that people living in the system are content with their lives. One way to look at the happiness aspect is to consider Maslow's (1943) hierarchy of needs (Figure 2). A person who has reached all five levels from the bottom to the top of the needs pyramid has satisfied all her physiological, safety, social, self-esteem and self-actualisation needs, and would therefore be considered a happy, content person.

Modern, wealthy societies have almost uniformly achieved the two lowest levels of the hierarchy. Most people have also reached the third level, having family and some friendships. When moving up to the last two levels, fewer individuals fit in. While achievement is much appreciated in Western societies, there is also constant pressure to perform, which can be deleterious to one's well-being. Work also tends to be quite specialised, which may not be consistent with creativity and spontaneity. On the other hand, schooling in wealthy Western societies lasts at least eight or nine years, more for most, providing ample opportunities for creativity and problem solving during that time. Subsequently, according to Maslow's hierarchy, modern capitalist systems should produce reasonably good results but by no means guarantee that their people are content with life.

**Figure 2    Maslow's hierarchy of needs**

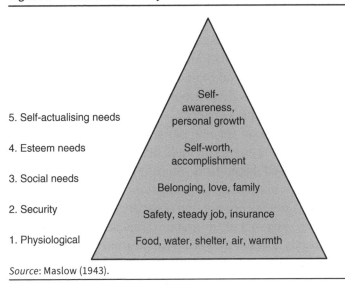

5. Self-actualising needs

4. Esteem needs

3. Social needs

2. Security

1. Physiological

Self-awareness, personal growth

Self-worth, accomplishment

Belonging, love, family

Safety, steady job, insurance

Food, water, shelter, air, warmth

*Source*: Maslow (1943).

Utopia also clearly satisfies the lowest two of Maslow's levels. The third level, social needs, is a particularly strong point for it. The forty-member family units are designed for close friendships, for a sense of belonging to a close-knit group, and for family needs in general. The fourth, esteem, level in Utopia rests largely on the possible satisfaction that a worker gets from other members of the group after fulfilling the daily work requirement. Esteem is also helped by job security built into the system. Some other needs of the fourth level, in particular independence, are clearly lacking in Utopia. At the fifth level, self-actualisation, there are two opposing forces in Utopia. Daily work for most people is tedious, far removed from attributes such as creativity or spontaneity. On the other hand, the production of necessities is the overriding goal of production, which has reduced the regular working day to six hours, after which there is special time dedicated to self-actualisation activities. In his later works Maslow (1969) included altruism and spirituality as additional important elements needed to satisfy one's highest needs. Both are certainly strong elements of Utopia's system.

To summarise the comparison, in terms of Maslow's system Utopia seems to hold its own against modern market-based capitalism. Since Maslow's hierarchy of needs does not place much weight on income or consumption, it is not surprising that a society with non-financial values scores well in the system. Some levels of need – social needs, esteem and self-actualisation – are not clearly associated with money. In contrast, capitalism has a built-in trait where self-interested individuals compete for property, winning and losing being an inherent part of the game. In Utopia exchanges are modeled on altruism, making the stressful part of private property exchanges disappear. In that respect, Utopia's common property institution is more compatible with Maslow's hierarchy than is private property–based capitalism.

## Conclusion

The findings of this study show how a small change in a society's institutional set-up can have a large effect on societal outcomes. The case of Utopia shows particularly well the multidimensionality of economic systems. No less than 500 years ago Sir Thomas More made common property the cornerstone institution in his *Utopia*. Yet common property is often looked down upon as a tool of economic development. This view was strengthened after the full socio-economic legacy of the Soviet Union had become clear: when everything belongs to everyone, it belongs to no one, taking away an individual's incentive to take care of the property and to be productive. The sorry state of property during the last few decades of socialism wiped away any substantive economic arguments in favour of common property–based systems.

Yet *Utopia* combines common property, strict internal rules, modern economic concepts and religious habits for a seemingly functional economic system. With a careful mixing of institutions and sound economic insights, More seems to have built a framework for a society that could also – unlike other large-scale constructs based on common property – be viable in the long run. While the conditions that make *Utopia* work out are quite restrictive (strong religious beliefs, altruism, small economic units, lives devoid of luxury, strict regulation of time use), it does provide a sketch of a society where common property may not stifle long-term development, but is associated with productive and happy people. (For an account of present-day experiments in living that approximate *Utopia*, see the appendix.)

## Appendix: The Hutterites

Utopia as proposed by More has never been tried on a national scale. Yet there are some present-day communities that share much with *Utopia*. The closest of them may be the Hutterites, a communal branch of Anabaptists. Followers of Jakob Hutter (d. 1536), an Austrian leader, they have built close to 500 colonies in North America, most of them in the western Canadian plains of Alberta, Saskatchewan and Manitoba. Each colony has between 60 and 200 people, which is considered the optimal size. After a colony reaches the optimal size, a new one is started at a fair distance from the existing ones. The Hutterites are strongly religious, have common property, wear simple, fairly uniform clothes, share common meals and have strong internal social norms and rules. Success in farming and ranching has made the colonies mostly self-sufficient. Their excess product is traded outside the colony, mostly through monetary transactions. The proceeds are used for buying production inputs (agricultural machinery) and services (mostly health-related) that cannot be produced within the colony. All children are educated within the colonies through the elementary grades, after which they are ready to assume full-time apprenticeships or jobs in the colony.

# 7 JUDAISM AND LIBERALISM: ISRAEL'S ECONOMIC PROBLEM WITH ITS HAREDIM

David Conway

## Judaism and liberalism

Judaism is an ancient religion with roots going back a thousand years before the cultures of ancient Greece and Rome. By contrast, liberalism is comparatively recent. There exists no systematic exposition of the political creed before the Reformation. The idea, therefore, that between the two there might be some intimate relation seems distinctly unpromising. All the more unpromising does any such connection seem given that, when liberalism made its first appearance in Europe as a political doctrine, Jews there were still very much a pariah people, banished to the margins of society and entirely without political influence or power (Maccoby 1996).

Nevertheless, through the unprecedented influence that, at the time of the Reformation, Jewish Scripture began to exert on the political imagination of some of Europe's profoundest thinkers and most energetic statesmen, the Jewish religion did play a decisive, albeit indirect, role in the emergence of liberalism. While the Old Testament had long formed part of the Christian canon, its understanding and status within the Roman Catholic Church was profoundly different from what it was for such champions of the Reformation as Luther and Calvin. As Eric Nelson (2011: 16) has noted in his study of the influence of Jewish Scripture upon sixteenth- and seventeenth-century European political thought:

> No longer regarding the Hebrew Bible as the Old Law – a shadowy intimation of the truth which had been rendered null and void by the New Dispensation ... in the wake of the Reformation ... [r]eaders began to see in the five books of Moses not just political wisdom, but a political constitution.

With the advent of the Reformation, the Pentateuch began to be viewed as a repository of political knowledge. However, this would not have given it then any prominent role in the emergence of liberalism had the Commonwealth that it portrays the ancient Israelites to have been under divine instruction to establish in Canaan not been suitably liberal in character. Clearly, it would have been a true miracle had this polity borne a perfect resemblance with any present-day secular liberal democracy. Such a form of political life was still too remote then even to have been capable of being comprehended, let alone embraced. In at least three respects, the constitution and laws of the ancient Hebrew Commonwealth are startlingly illiberal as judged by present-day standards. First, the worship of other gods was not just proscribed, but a capital offence (Deut. 17: 2–5). Second, as practically everywhere else at the time, slavery was uncritically accepted, albeit in a somewhat mitigated form. Third, some of its prescribed punishments seem decidedly barbaric: for example, the hand had to be cut off a married woman who had used it in an attempt to assist her husband in a fight by seizing the genitals of his combatant (Deut. 25: 1–12).

For their time, however, the laws and constitutional arrangements that Hebrew Scripture relates the ancient Israelites as having been under divine instruction to instate in their Commonwealth were remarkably forward-looking and liberal. Hence, the account given of them in those Scriptures had a huge attraction for those early moderns who sought to challenge prevailing illiberal orthodoxies.

Consider, for example, what was said about the ancient Hebrew Commonwealth at the time of the American Revolution by Samuel Langdon, president of Harvard University. In a speech to the Congress of Massachusetts, Langdon declared that, shorn of its ceremonial law: 'The civil polity of Israel was doubtless an excellent general model [of government]' (Eidelberg 2005).

To illustrate just how liberal in character the laws and constitution of that ancient Hebrew Commonwealth eventually came to be viewed, consider the account of their character that was given in a set of commentaries on them, published in America in 1853, by the Presbyterian minister E. C. Wines, one-time president of the City University of St Louis. He writes there that (Wines 1853: iv, 116–17, 115–18 *passim*):

The civil government of the ancient Hebrews was the government of a free people ... its constitution was pervaded with ... the spirit of liberty.

That government is instituted for the good of the many ... for the happiness of the people, and not the advantage of princes and nobles; that the people, either directly or by representatives, should have a voice in the enactment of the laws; that the powers of the several departments of government should be cautiously balanced; that the laws should be equal in their operation ... that the life, liberty, and property of no citizen could be infringed, but by process of law ... that judicial proceedings should be public, and conducted in accordance with established rules; that every man who obeys the laws, has a right to their protection; that education, embracing a knowledge of the laws, the obligations of citizenship, and the duties of morality, should be universal ... these great and vital principles of civil liberty were as fully embodied in the Hebrew constitution, as they are in the freest constitution now existing among men.

It is not in Greece that liberty was cradled... rather in that admirable frame of government given by the oracle of Jehovah ... that we find the type and model of our own constitution. Even the Declaration of American Independence ... was but an echo from the deep thunders of Mount Sinai.

For a long time, both before and after Wines wrote these remarks, the Hebraic provenance of liberalism was a commonplace. This is well illustrated by the observation made in a *History of the Hebrew Commonwealth*, published in 1920, of the contemporary poignancy of which its joint authors could have had no inkling at the time (Bailey and Kent 1920: 13–14):

> Under the iron heel of [the great military despotisms of Egypt, Babylonia, Assyria, and Persia] there grew and blossomed a tiny flower ... of human freedom [and] of the rights of man ... In time, the[se] ideals ... were expressed in definite laws, and all later democratic legislation is largely an unfolding of what is there set forth in principle.

Later, the in many ways remarkably liberal and forward-looking character of the original Hebraic Commonwealth came to be forgotten, being only lately rediscovered by a new generation of scholars of so-called Political Hebraism of whom the most notable are Fania Oz-Salzberger (2002, 2006), Yoram Hazony (2005), Yechiel Leiter (2008) and Joshua Berman (2008).

Meanwhile, liberalism has come to assume a welter of different, mutually conflicting, forms of which not all are as equally accommodating of, and friendly towards, economic freedom. My aim is to decide with which of these different varieties of contemporary liberalism Judaism may be considered to be in closest accord.

## The principal varieties of contemporary liberalism

For purposes of comparison, I propose to arrange the principal contemporary varieties of liberalism into three basic groups which I will respectively term *libertarianism, classical liberalism* and *social liberalism*. The chief differences between the members of the three groups pertain to the respectively different conceptions they each have of the legitimate role of government.

*Libertarianism* denies the need for, and moral legitimacy of, any more extensive form of government than the bare minimum provided by the legendary *night-watchman state* whose sole function is to protect the lives, liberty and property of those over whom it exercises authority. *Classical liberalism* and *social liberalism* each affirm the need for, and legitimacy of, more extensive government than the mere minimum provided by the night-watchman state. However, they differ in their views of how much more is needed and on why. There are two principal varieties of libertarianism. One favours the minimum government provided by the night-watchman state and hence is sometimes termed *minarchy* (Nozick 1974). The other, sometimes referred to as *anarcho-capitalism*, denies the need and legitimacy for even that much government (Rothbard 1973; Friedman 1973; Hoppe 1989). According to its advocates, there is no useful function that any government performs that could not be still more effectively and equitably provided by commercial corporations or other voluntary bodies such as charities.

According to *classical liberalism*, over and above the protection of persons and their property, there is a further range of so-called *public goods* beyond the protection of life, liberty and property whose public provision is both desirable and warranted. This is because, according to it, all societal members benefit from their provision at a level beyond such as would be provided them were it left entirely to the market and other voluntary bodies. The main proponents of classical liberalism are John Locke, Adam Smith, John Stuart Mill and more latterly Ludwig von Mises, Friedrich Hayek and Milton Friedman. Still more recent exponents of classical liberalism as construed here are Loren Lomasky, and still more recently that set of contemporary American political philosophers who sail under the colours of self-styled *bleeding-heart libertarianism*. These latter include such political theorists as Matt Zwolinski, John Tomasi, Daniel Shapiro and Mike Rappaport.

The canonical statement and justification of the role of government favoured by classical liberalism was given by Adam Smith in the *Wealth of Nations*, where he called political arrangement established through his favoured role for government 'the system of natural liberty' and which he described so (Smith 1776, IV. 9. 51):

> According to the system of natural liberty, the sovereign has only three duties to attend to ... first, the duty of protecting the society from the violence and invasion of other independent societies; secondly, the duty of protecting, as far as possible, every member of the society from the injustice of oppression of every other member of it, or the duty of establishing an exact administration of justice; and thirdly, the duty of erecting and maintaining certain

public works and certain public institutions, which it can never be for the interest of any individual, or small number of individuals, to erect and maintain; because the profit could never repay the expense to any individual or small number of individuals, though it may frequently do much more than repay it to a great society.

Among those public goods of which (for the reason adumbrated above) classical liberalism favours the public provision, there are two with which we shall shortly be preoccupied: assistance to the poor, better today known as welfare, and basic education. In contrast with both libertarianism and classical liberalism, *social liberalism* favours their public provision in still even greater measure and for different reasons than does classical liberalism. In addition, social liberalism supports many forms of governmental activity for which classical liberalism, like libertarianism, sees neither the need nor any legitimacy (Rawls 1971). Social liberalism perceives the need and legitimacy for the public provision of all these goods to arise from moral demands that, it claims, emanate from the equal moral status of all societal members. Chief among such moral demands, so it claims, is a moral obligation that society has to ensure that none of its members enjoy any less favourable life chances than any others without their deserving to. Rather than reduce the life chances of society's better-endowed members so as to equalise those of every societal member, social liberalism supports redistributive and other public measures designed to maximise the life chances of society's least well-endowed members.

The equal moral status of all societal members is acknowledged by both libertarianism and classical liberalism, but they deny that any such strongly egalitarian moral demands on society follow from such equality.

My aim now is to decide with which of the three varieties of liberalism distinguished above Judaism may be considered in closest accord. My decision will be based on two sets of considerations: first, the laws and constitutional arrangements that the Pentateuch relates the Israelites to have been divinely instructed through Moses to institute in their Commonwealth; second, the later rabbinic teachings concerning the legitimate role of public authorities based on the divine laws relayed to the Israelites according to the Pentateuch.

## Why it is with classical liberalism that Judaism is in closest accord

The principal thesis for which I will now seek to argue is that the species of liberalism with which Judaism is in closest accord is classical liberalism.

Anarcho-capitalism may be judged to be incongruent with Judaism on the strength of the instruction which the Pentateuch reports Moses issuing the Israelites to: 'Pick from each of your tribes men who are wise, discerning, and experienced to serve as your heads' (Deut. 19: 13). By so issuing it, Moses may be said to have personally awarded representative government his own *hechsher*.[1]

---

1   A *hechsher* is a special stamp or marking placed by rabbinic authorities on packages of products to certify that they conform to the requirements of Jewish law.

Other constitutional arrangements and laws that the Pentateuch reports God as similarly instructing Moses to command the Israelites to instate in their Commonwealth (as their freely chosen covenantal ruler) render minarchy and social liberalism equally incongruent with Judaism. The most notable of such laws and arrangements are those that mandate assistance to the poor and a basic education for all Israelites within the Hebrew Commonwealth. It is these legal provisions that render Judaism in closest accord with classical liberalism. This is because, among all the varieties of liberalism, it is only classical liberalism that advocates publicly funded assistance to the poor and universal publicly funded basic schooling in such similarly restrained and discriminating a manner as they are mandated to be provided in the Hebrew Bible and in later rabbinic teachings.

Such welfare and educational policies have been advocated by practically all classical liberals from John Locke, Adam Smith and John Stuart Mill through to Friedrich Hayek and Milton Friedman. Even Ludwig von Mises supported public poor relief, he who is rightly regarded as having been the most libertarian of classical liberals and who, Milton Friedman recounts, once stormed out of a meeting at the very first Mont Pelerin Society Congress in 1947 after accusing his interlocutors, including Friedman, of being 'a bunch of socialists' (Friedman 1991: 18). Mises wrote: 'It is true that liberal politicians have striven against the encouragement of beggars by means of indiscriminate alms giving ... But they have never protested against support through the Poor Law of people unable to work' (Mises 1951: 467). 'No ordered community has callously allowed the poor and incapacitated to starve. There has always been some sort of institution designed to save from destitution people unable to sustain themselves' (Mises 1951: 475).

## Welfare provision as mandated in the Hebrew Bible

The chief constitutional arrangement in the Hebrew Commonwealth mandated to secure a basic education to all was the denial to the Levites of any tribal agricultural land of their own, unlike as was assigned to all the other Israelite tribes. Instead, the other Israelites were under divine instruction to support the Levites through various forms of payment. Among these required payments, the chief one was an annual tithe of a tenth of their agricultural produce. In return for it, the Levites were under divine ordinance to undertake several public offices of which the chief one, after ritual worship at the Temple, was to provide the other Israelites with an education in their national history and divinely ordained law (Num. 18: 21; Deut. 33:10).

The Levites discharged their educative function partly in Jerusalem during the three major festivals that all Israelites were annually required to celebrate there. However, the Levites mainly fulfilled their role as educators while resident in the 48 cities especially set aside for them, four cities to each of the 12 tribal territories, in which they would usually have been resident for the greater part of each year. As Joshua Berman (1995: 63–86 *passim*) has observed:

> [T]he primary purpose of the tithes and priestly gifts was not to support them in their role as sanctuary officiants, but to enable them to devote themselves to the study and dissemination of the Torah ... The tithing system creates a system of support for the Levites which allows them to devote themselves to mastery of God's laws. As masters of God's laws, it follows that they should serve ... as teachers of those laws ...

The chief laws within the Hebrew Commonwealth designed to ensure that assistance was given to the poor were those that endowed them with entitlement to food in various ways. These laws included: those that permitted them to glean the corners of fields at harvest time and that farmers were prohibited from harvesting; to gather what these farmers had harvested but forgotten to take from fields or else had accidentally dropped there; as well as those permitting them to help themselves to whatever these fields spontaneously yielded during their mandatory fallow, seventh sabbatical year. These laws also included the triennial tithe on agricultural produce that farmers were required to provide the poor in the third and sixth years of the seven-year cycle.

Some have denied that these laws, and those similarly mandating public support of the Levites, to have been anything but unenforceable religious ordinances that called only for voluntary acts of individual charity, rather than having had the status of enforceable and enforced civic ordinances (Lifshitz 2004; Paley 2006). The case for so regarding these laws is weak. While the mechanisms for their enforcement might well have been weak and often ineffectual, there is biblical warrant for supposing the laws mandating assistance to the poor and support of the Levites to have been considered enforceable and originally enforced. The warrant comes from the book of Job, widely thought to have been composed during the Second Commonwealth although set in the pre-Commonwealth times of Abraham. In that book, the sorely troubled Job is reported as looking back with yearning on his former life before it went awry and stating (Job 29: 2–17):

> Oh that I were as in ... the days gone by when God watched over me [and] I was in my prime ... When I passed through the city gates to take my seat in the square, young men saw me and hid, elders rose and stood, nobles held back their words ... For I saved the poor man who cried out [and] the orphan who had none to help him ... I gladdened the heart of the widow ... Justice was my cloak and turban ... I was a father to the needy ... I looked into the case of the stranger. I broke the jaws of the wrongdoer.

What Job here seems to be describing is his former role as an elder engaged in the civic enforcement of those laws that mandated public assistance to the poor, and with which readers of the book could be presumed to be familiar from the Pentateuch (Mason 1987, 1992). That the welfare provision mandated in the Hebrew Bible should be regarded as required public provision rather than commendatory private, voluntary charitable giving is also the view of Robert A. Oden Jr. Drawing on a definition of taxation supplied by the Israeli jurist Menachem Elon, Oden (1984: 163) observes of the welfare provision as mandated in the Hebrew Bible:

> According to this definition ... 'tax is a compulsory payment ... exacted by a public authority, for the purpose of satisfying the latter's own needs or those of the public, or part of the public.' ... [As] so defined taxation is a phenomenon met often and in many forms within ancient Israel.

Oden (1984: 168–69) further remarks that:

> The provisions for the Sabbatical Year, the Jubilee Year, and the gleaning rights all represent welfare taxation systems according to which landowners and slave-owners are required to give up income they might otherwise expect for the benefit of those classes otherwise without protection in ancient Israel.

## Welfare provision as mandated in rabbinic Judaism

There is further, post-biblical warrant for supposing the status of the divine requirements of the Israelites to provide welfare to the poor and a basic education to all to have had the status of enforceable laws rather than private acts of supererogation. It comes from the arrangements which Jewish communities routinely instituted to secure assistance to the poor and a basic religious education to all Jews, during the many centuries that they lived as self-contained, self-governing, communities, with their own powers of taxation and law enforcement. As the Israeli jurist and one-time Supreme Court Justice Menachem Elon (1975) has explained:

> From the close of the geonic period onward [c. 1000 CE], Jewish autonomy found its main expression in the various Jewish communal organisations or in a roof organisation embracing a number of communities ... The community provided various social services and maintained religious, educational, and judicial institutions, as well as its own administrative and governing bodies, all of which had to be financed through various methods of taxation ... The purposes for which taxes were levied during the post-talmudic period embraced a wide spectrum of municipal needs – such as maintaining the town guard, providing health, educational and religious services, and for judicial and civic ... institutions ... [and] funds for charity to the poor ... in addition to various taxes ... imposed by the central authorities on the Jewish community and collected by the communal authorities from its members.

With full rabbinic approval, Jewish communities routinely exercised their powers of taxation to impose and enforce compulsory levies to raise communal funds with which to provide assistance to the poor and compulsory schooling for all children. As was remarked by the one-time senior economist at the Bank of Israel, Meir Tamari (1987: 242–43, 210–11):

> [R]ight from the outset, Judaism understood that it was the community's duty to provide for the social needs of the individuals in that community ... [T]hroughout the centuries and irrespective of which countries they inhabited, Jews have maintained a widely ramified welfare system, in its most modern sense.

> It must be stressed that the financing of these services bore all the hallmarks of government activity; that they were, in fact, undertaken by autonomous communities is irrelevant. For the individual Jew, these communities had all the authority and power to tax and punish evasion that the state has today ... The setting up of a tax system ... made participation in communal financing obligatory in addition to the voluntary charitable acts demanded by Judaism from the individual.

In biblical and post-biblical times, the communal arrangements instituted for welfare and education succeeded in avoiding the moral hazards that have bedevilled the manner in which these two public goods have been provided by the overblown welfare states of today. In biblical times, the agricultural laws giving the poor title to food required them to work to obtain it. The triennial tithe is likely to have been reserved for those poor too old or infirm to work, or else for when gleanings were insufficient to meet the basic subsistence needs of the able-bodied poor. As Mason (1987: 6) has observed:

> The third-year tithe provision ... probably was restricted to those who could not be expected to conduct the effort necessary for gleaning; or perhaps it was available for the dependent [poor, i.e. those who, for whatever reasons (childcare responsibilities, disablement, age), cannot realistically be expected to work for remuneration in order to subsist] when the gleanings were not sufficient or available ... If it is assumed that different *beth'avoth* [economically viable (i.e. propertied) extended-families] supplying the tithe were on separate tithe cycles, which is the most economically plausible rendering ... then there would be an amount available every year for relief of this type.

In post-biblical times, access to communal funds was rigorously means-tested and work demanded of all its able-bodied recipients. Wherever possible, the overriding aim of communities was to restore the poor to economic independence as quickly as possible. Better still, it was to prevent anyone from falling into poverty in the first place, by means of timely job offers and interest-free loans that provided individuals with plenty of opportunities for individual acts of charity. Furthermore, families were expected to support impoverished relatives before the latter were eligible for communal support. As F. M. Lowenberg (2001: 13, 17) has noted:

Ancient Judea was not a welfare state in the modern meaning of the term, but it was a society that was vitally concerned with the welfare of all who lived within its borders. It cannot be suggested that its government provided a wide range of services that were designed to contribute to the well-being of the nation. Yet this society was so concerned with the fate of its poor and dependants that it made institutional provision for their care ... Greeks, and later Romans, felt responsible for members of their own family, and for those who resided in their *polis*, but did not feel any responsibility for foreigners. Of all ancient people only the Jews felt responsible for the plight of all *poor*, both for family members and strangers.

Similarly, in the case of education, the arrangements for its public provision in the First Hebrew Commonwealth avoided the worst excesses associated with its public provision today. This was achieved by its being left to the discretion of payers of the annual tithe to the Levites to which specific Levites they gave it. Later on, after these original communal arrangements for education had broken down, the successor arrangements for the provision of education managed also to avoid the moral hazards associated with its public provision today. Jewish communities reserved the right to hire and fire at will their communally appointed teachers. Additionally, communities actively encouraged prospective teachers to come forward and compete for posts already occupied against their incumbents. As Meir Tamari (1987: 273–4) remarks:

Joseph Caro, in the *Shulchan Arukh* [a widely accepted code of Jewish law drawn up in the sixteenth century], authoritatively lays [it] down that if a community finds a more qualified teacher, then it is permitted to remove the present one from the post ... Furthermore, competition between teachers and rabbis was actively encouraged, according to the [Talmudic] dictum 'The jealousy of scribes [scholars] increases wisdom.' Even those authorities who opposed competitive practices in general agreed to a relaxation of such barriers in the case of teachers and rabbis ... communities endeavoured to attract great scholars to settle in their midst, offering not only direct salaries but other forms of financial assistance ... a man was not allowed to dwell in a town or community that did not provide Torah education for its children.

All in all, the arrangements and laws for welfare and education that Jews have instituted on the basis of their religion, in both biblical and post-biblical times, render their religion more closely in accord in outlook with the tenets of classical liberalism than they do with those of either of the two other principal varieties of contemporary liberalism. This is because these laws and arrangements accord more closely with the public arrangements that classical liberalism favours for the provision of education and welfare than with those arrangements, if any, that are favoured for them by either of the two other principal varieties of liberalism.

## The present-day relevance of Judaism's affinity with classical liberalism

Some might wonder what value there can possibly be in establishing with which variety of contemporary liberalism Judaism most closely accords. What matters, they might be imagined as saying, is only which variety of liberalism is the soundest, not which is most in accord with Mosaic edicts originally designed for entirely different times and circumstances. Such a reaction would be in order were the biblical laws at the core of Judaism not still considered to be binding, and eternally so, by those Jews in Israel today who have it within their power to do more there to promote economic freedom than practically anybody else. This they could do were they only to decide to live in accord with what has here been argued to have been the true spirit and intent of those biblical laws that relate to the provision of welfare and education. I refer to Israel's ultra-orthodox Jews, the so-called Haredim (literally meaning: 'tremblers' in fear of God). Their singular ability these past several decades to exploit the leverage that was inadvertently given them by their country's defective system of national proportional representation is steadily bleeding that nation dry in welfare benefits and educational subsidies, which are ultimately as unsustainable as they are divisive. As has been noted by Eli Berman (2000: 916, 942–43), professor of economics at the University of California:

> Families with fathers in *yeshivas* are extremely dependent on government support. Only 18 per cent of family

income is earned, almost entirely from the wife's earnings ... [T]ransfers mostly from the government account for at least 70 per cent of the income for these families, not including pensions, disability, and other National Insurance programs.

In order to maintain this standard of living at current levels of *yeshiva* attendance and ultra-orthodox fertility, outside support of the community would have to continue to increase at 4–5 per cent annually or double 16–18 years, a growth rate much higher than Israel's rate of per capita output growth. At current levels of transfers and taxes, the ultra-orthodox population growth rate will make Israel's welfare system insolvent and bankrupt municipalities with large ultra-orthodox populations. The status quo is not sustainable without transferring an increased proportion of output to welfare programs.

Despite Israel's recent so-called economic miracle, the economic threat that its Haredim pose to it, identified by Eli Berman back in 2000, has not abated. Dan Senor and Saul Singer remarked on it in their 2009 book *Start-Up Nation: The Story of Israel's Economic Miracle*, where they observed that: 'Of all the threats and challenges facing Israel, an inability to keep the economy growing is perhaps the greatest' (Senor and Singer 2009: 223). Drawing on the opinion of Israeli macro-economist Dan Ben-David, the threat the Haredim pose to Israel, according to Senor and Singer (2009: 220), is created by their:

... low participation in the economy. A little over half Israel's workforce contributes to the economy in a productive way, compared to 65 percent in the United States. The low Israeli workforce participation rate is chiefly attributable to [its] *haredim*, or the ultra-orthodox Jews ... Among mainstream Israeli Jewish civilians aged twenty-five to sixty-four ... 84 percent of men... are employed. Among ... *haredi* men ... 73 percent respectively are *not* employed.

In an address delivered one year into his presidency of Israel in June 2015, Reuven Rivlin reiterated the severe threat that its Haredim continue to pose to the viability of Israel as a developed, liberal democracy, when he remarked that (Rivlin 2015):

In the 1990s, Israeli society comprised ... a large secular Zionist majority, and beside it three minority groups: a national-religious [i.e. modern orthodox] minority, an Arab minority and a Haredi minority ... Today, the first grade classes are composed of about 38 per cent secular Jews, about 15 per cent national-religious, about one quarter Arabs, and close to a quarter Haredim ... [T]he distribution into four principal tribes that make up Israeli society [today] ... for many of us is ... a threat to the secular-liberal character of the State of Israel ... From an economic viewpoint, the current reality is not viable ... If we do not reduce the current gaps in the rate of participation in the work force ... of the Arab and Haredi populations – who are soon to become one half of the work force – Israel will not be able to continue to be a developed economy.

A major contributory cause of the threat that Israel's Arab and Haredi populaces pose to it derives from their very low labour force participation rate. 'According to the Central Bureau of Statistics [of Israel], 61% of Haredi women work (88% of secular women) compared to only 52% of Haredi men (93% of secular men). The National Economic Council states that the employment rate among Haredi women is 57% and 40.4% among Haredi men' (Maimon and Rosner 2013).

In the case of Haredi men, a large part of the cause of their economic inactivity has been the exemption Haredi publicly funded schools have been able to obtain from having to teach the secular subjects (like English and mathematics) that form the otherwise mandatory core curriculum in all Israeli schools in receipt of public funding. The result has been to leave their alumni practically unemployable in a modern economy and hence locked into a pattern of life that requires their male graduates to continue their economic inactivity through perpetual religious study at public expense. Their exemption from normal employment requirements, combined with very generous levels of child support, has led Israel's Haredi population to mushroom at ever greater public expense. As has been noted (Klemon 2012):

Estimates put the Haredi population in Israel as low as one-in-ten and as high as one-in-six ... Due to their high

> birth rates, when broken down by age group, the Haredi
> make up an even larger sizable proportion to secular chil-
> dren studying in an Israeli primary or secondary school.
> It is reported that as few as 40 per cent of these haredi
> schools are even teaching English or math.

The impending economic consequences seem disastrous, as Hirsh Goodman notes in in his 2011 book *The Anatomy of Israel's Survival*: 'The religious school system ... created with government funding [has] failed to prepare their chil-dren for the real world. It [has] concentrated only on reli-gious education, thereby perpetuating the cycle of poverty and state dependence' (Goodman 2011: 219).

It is Israel's Haredim above all who need to be made to realise that the kind of society that most accords with the injunctions of their religion would demand of all but a few persons economic self-reliance in adulthood, rather than publicly funded, permanent full-time study. Such a society would also be willing to support their schools financially only if they were to follow a national core curriculum that rendered their students employable upon leaving them, and had forged bonds between them and other Israelis through the common consciousness instilled by a com-mon core curriculum. No one ever better explained the invaluable civic role that was performed in creating and maintaining unity among Jews, initially by the Levites and later by communally maintained schools, than did Moses Angel, head for more than half a century during the Victo-rian period of the Jews' Free School in London. In his book *The Law of Sinai*, Angel (1858: 92–93) observed:

> Composed as the land of Israel was of several distinct territories, appropriated to the different tribes, there was every reason but one that a diversity of customs and interests should gradually spring up, and that the country should resemble ancient Greece in the number of its commonwealths than remain an undivided government. That one reason was the existence of the priesthood ... Penetrating the entire country, carrying out everywhere the exposition of the same principles ... the priesthood preserved a uniformity of customs and a community of interests ... When after the dispersion, the priestly function ceased, the first care of the Jewish leaders was to provide for that ministration now rendered considerably more necessary by the dissolution of the national existence ... Wherever Jews dwelt, therefore, there existed numerous schools, yeshivas and bet midroshim [houses of study] ... And thus as widespread as the Jews themselves was the knowledge of their sacred duties, and the rabbis ... taught and expounded the doctrines which their predecessors, the priests, had preserved.

Many of the greatest early classical liberals, including John Locke, Adam Smith and John Stuart Mill, similarly emphasised the need for such common associative bonds as alone the exposure of all young to a common curriculum can provide as essential conditions of any viable civil society. Accordingly they supported the public provision of elementary schooling, in part for the express purpose of creating a common national consciousness, something all too conspicuously lacking in present-day Israel. For example, John Stuart Mill (1861: 430–31) wrote in his late essay *Considerations on Representative Government* that:

> Free institutions are next to impossible in a country ... [whose] people [are] without fellow-feeling ... The influences which form opinions and decide political acts, are different in the different sections of the country. An altogether different set of leaders have the confidence of one part of the country and of another. The same books, newspapers, pamphlets, speeches do not reach them ... Their mutual antipathies are generally much stronger than [their] jealousy of the government.

The kind of national disunity that Mill argued here to be incompatible with free institutions is precisely what Israel's Haredim are in process there of deliberately creating through their separatist schools that deny their pupils any common curriculum with that taught in Israel's other schools. Quite apart from the economic strains which their unemployable graduates are imposing on the rest of Israeli society, the resulting disunity in Israel could be fatal to it as a Jewish democratic state, as has been noted by David Gordis (2011), who observes that:

> The Jews have successfully recreated the kingdom of the Bible's dreams ... Political stability must be laboriously maintained [however]; decline and destruction are always a danger ... We must be re-inspired to seek the grand destiny, made possible by nation-states, and guard them closely, lest they crumble and fall, taking with them

the unique form of human flourishing that is possible only when a people dwells free, in its own land.

The irony is that communally supported religious education, which started out being such a powerful and effective device among Jews for creating and preserving solidarity and cohesion among them, should have become today in Israel, of all places, such a potent source of division and animosity between them. The 'Scholar Society' which Israel's Haredim have been intent on creating for themselves there is as much at variance with authentic Judaism as it is with sound economics. As the aptly named Israeli scholar Noam Zion has observed in his 2012 pamphlet *The Ethics of Economics: Israeli-Haredim and Israeli Arabs – The Duty to Work and the Duty to Provide Work* (Zion 2012: 7–11 *passim*):

> The Haredi leadership in Israel ... defends its communal policies that discourage work and the learning of marketable skills by men ... argu[ing] that those who study Torah full-time are a spiritual elite who serve God in the name of the community. However the social revolution after World War Two [which started with the introduction into Israel in 1949 of free, compulsory education] was to raise the percentage of Haredi men engaged in lifelong study from 5% to 90%, regardless of their level of talent or the needs of the community for their service ...

> [Jewish] law may well have regarded the teachers and elite halakhic scholars as exempt [from being obligated to pay their fair share for economic benefits] because of

their communal service just as ... the cantor ought to be exempt. But not those studying for their own sake ... [M]ost of the Talmudic rabbis were themselves skilled labourers ... Maimonides wrote passionately against rabbinic parasitism: 'The greatest rabbis were cutters of wood [Hillel], carriers of beams and drawers of water for gardens, blacksmiths and makers of coal; rather than asking the public for aid and even when the public gave them [tzedakah], they refused to accept it. One should always pressure oneself and manage somehow with privation (distress) rather than be dependent upon other people or cast oneself upon the public [by asking for tzedukah].' [*Mishneh Torah*, Gifts to the Poor, 10: 18.] 'No labour should be considered beneath one's station when the alternative is exploiting communal charity.' Rabbi Aharon of Lunel (14th century Provenance, France): 'It is disgusting before God to be one who benefits from the tzedakah fund because s/he would rather not make an effort to benefit from his/her own labour' ... Judah HaHasid (Germany, 13th century): 'If you encounter a pauper who ... is suited to learn ... [a gainful skill] yet refuses to make the effort, the person is unworthy of tzedakah.' Rabbi Yechiel bar Yekutiel (13th century, Rome): 'Just as people are expected to care for their own interests, so the poor are expected not to impose themselves ... on the community, except in extreme circumstances ... One who depends on the community dole is stealing from the poor. It is entirely fit and proper to withhold support from such a person and to shame them into seeking employment.' Rabbi Shimshon Rafael Hirsch ... a major leader and inspiration for separatist Haredi Orthodoxy in Germany and Middle Europe in the 19th century ... sees in job training not just a pragmatic solution to financial needs but a 'calling', a profession, a vocation, to support oneself ... a mitzvah [divine command].

Apropos the impending welfare crisis facing Israel on account of its long-standing overindulgence of its Haredim, they would all do well were they to be reminded of an adage made famous by Milton Friedman. Adapting it to the present context, the adage would run: There is no such thing as a free Kiddush, nor a perpetual Talmud *shiur* either. The sooner Israel's Haredim can be made to appreciate that this elementary economic insight is also the teaching of their religion, the better will it be for all Israel.

# 8 THE TRUE MEANING OF 'SOCIAL JUSTICE': A CATHOLIC VIEW OF HAYEK

Martin Rhonheimer

## The problem of social justice talk

*Social justice* has become a term which is in everybody's mouth but is hardly ever defined. The term appeals to widely shared feelings and intuitions concerning justice, and therefore seems to be self-explanatory. Such feelings mostly refer to different kinds of inequality which are perceived as unjust.

These feelings and intuitions are not just vain or lacking any sound basis. Nor do I want simply to identify them with sentiments of envy, even though in many cases envy certainly plays a role. However, I think that the ubiquity of social justice talk originates in a moral intuition which should be taken seriously. The popularity of the term seems to lie in the fact that social and economic inequalities are no longer accepted as fate, or God-given, or imposed by nature. In a dynamic world of unprecedented economic growth driven by human endeavour, the inequalities generated are also seen as caused by human beings.

The sound moral intuitions underlying claims for social justice are, however, mostly misguided by ignorance of the real causes of wealth and economic growth as well as of basic facts of economics such as the scarcity of resources and the role of capital accumulation, especially its decisive importance for technological innovation and consequent rise in productivity and general prosperity. These moral intuitions are, moreover, misguided by a misapprehension of the limited reach of human knowledge and of the nature and importance of markets in overcoming these limitations, as well as by myths concerning economic history, especially a sometimes far-reaching misreading of the history of capitalism.

Social justice is commonly conceived to be *justice of distribution*, or, as it is traditionally called, *distributive justice*. According to tradition, distributive justice is to be distinguished from commutative justice, the justice of relations between individual human beings, such as in buying and selling and every kind of contract. Distributive justice is the justice in dealings of superior communities or authorities, namely the state, with single persons posited under their authority or command. Distributive justice refers to the just distribution of burdens (e.g. taxation) and of benefits (not only material but also immaterial, e.g. honours).

One of the fiercest and most influential critics of the concept of social justice has been F. A. Hayek. Hayek himself follows the common usage of understanding social justice simply as distributive justice. This narrowing of the perspective prevents Hayek from taking into account other possible meanings of social justice which, as we will see, are fully compatible with his critique of social justice as distributive justice and with his views on the market.

In the following I first set out Hayek's critique of social justice, focusing on the merits of this critique but also its limitations. These limitations lead us, in a second step, to a set of questions ignored by Hayek and other libertarian critics of social justice and thus to a widening of the perspective. Third, I elaborate a higher-order concept of social justice that encapsulates our most authentic moral intuitions about justice and is compatible with both anthropological principles of Catholic social doctrine and Hayek's position. Finally, I examine how such an outlook can be integrated into Catholic social doctrine. This involves discussing some misunderstandings among Catholics about the role of markets; this discussion will confirm Hayek's main points, while integrating them into a wider perspective.

## Hayek's criticism of social justice

For Hayek it is crucial to understand societies, markets and the legal systems in which markets are embedded as examples of spontaneous order. This does not mean a naturally evolving order, that is, one free from intervention by human decisions or steering by politicians, lawyers and legislators. According to Hayek, spontaneous orders are to be distinguished from orders which are designed intentionally for a determinate purpose, something which is typical for organisations. Societies, markets and legal systems which contain a great multitude of individuals with diverging preferences and therefore pursuing different ends are not established like organisations, but arise as the result of evolutionary processes which are not intentionally designed for a determined end. The rules and institutional principles shaping such spontaneous orders can assure cooperation between individuals pursuing different ends, avoiding the subordination of the legitimate freedom of individuals to the dominant preferences of others. The only spontaneous orders compatible with freedom are, therefore, those governed by legal rules which are open to an indeterminate range of outcomes and not intentionally designed to bring about a determined end or state of affairs.

Free market economies develop as spontaneous orders. They are the proper economic order of a free society. Their distributional outcomes are not organised, planned or otherwise guided by any intentional design. Therefore, and this is Hayek's main point in his *The Mirage of Social Justice*, the outcomes of markets can be called neither 'just' nor 'unjust': 'only human conduct can be called just or unjust' (Hayek 1976: 31). Hayek affirms: 'In a free society in which the position of the different individuals and groups is not the result of anybody's design ... the differences in reward simply cannot meaningfully be described as just or unjust' (1976: 70). The market does not act with a single intention or purpose; it is not an actor at all. Therefore, the moral specifications of 'just' and 'unjust' cannot be applied to its distributional results.

While admitting that 'We are of course not wrong when we perceive that the effects on the different individuals and groups of the economic processes of a free society are not distributed according to some recognizable principle of justice', Hayek argues that we cannot conclude 'that they are unjust and that someone is responsible and to be blamed for this' (1976: 83). We cannot treat society or the market as a single, intentional agent responsible for the outcome of its actions. Provided we abhor the command economy of socialism and a totalitarian political system, and understand that a market economy is 'a system in which each is allowed to use his knowledge for his own purposes', that is, the economic order of a free society, then 'the concept of "social justice" is necessarily empty and meaningless, because in it nobody's will can determine the relative incomes of the different people, or prevent that they be partly dependent on accident' (1976: 69).

In addition to the clear insight into the nature of the market economy and the conditions for a free society that is at the root of Hayek's view, his conception of the economic life, of cooperation and society, is deeply humanistic; it is based on the primacy of the individual person and his or her liberty and self-responsibility. Hayek is far from indifferent towards persons who are not capable of taking part in what he calls the 'catallactic game' of the market. Such persons must be assisted or taken care of by the entire community, he says, if necessary by an 'assured minimum income, or a floor below which nobody need to descend'; such an insurance against extreme misfortune 'may well be in the interest of all; or it may be felt to be a clear moral duty of all to assist, within the organized community, those who cannot help themselves' (1976: 87).[1]

---

1   See also Hayek (1960: 257 f., 286). A. J. Tebble (2009) has argued that this
    claim is inconsistent with the philosophical underpinnings of Hayek's
    liberalism. I cannot discuss here Tebble's arguments. My own critique of
    Hayek, however, seems to me to resolve a possible problem of inconsistency,
    while leaving substantially intact Hayek's rejection of 'social justice'.

However, Hayek makes another point which, in my opinion, is crucial in the present context, although he does not develop it further. He admits that 'If we apply the terms [just or unjust] to a *state of affairs*, they have meaning only in so far as we hold *someone responsible for bringing it about or allowing it to come about*' (1976: 31; emphasis added). This statement has far-reaching consequences. Hayek repeats the point two pages later: 'Since only situations which have been created by human will can be called just or unjust, the particulars of a spontaneous order cannot be just or unjust: *if it is not the intended or foreseen result of somebody's action ... this cannot be called just or unjust*' (1976: 33; emphasis added).

Markets are certainly spontaneous orders, not only in the way they have developed over time but also in the way they work at any given time. However, even if the outcomes of their catallactic processes are not intended by any single human actor, they always produce their outcomes in the context of a given legal and institutional framework for whose continuing existence determinate persons actually *are* responsible. Determinate legal and institutional arrangements as well as a particular property distribution may very well lead the spontaneous order of the market to produce distributional results – for example, inequalities or disadvantage and discrimination against particular groups of people – which under *different* legal and institutional preconditions would not have been produced this way. For example, if a legal order discriminates against determinate social, ethnic or religious groups, depriving them from the possibility of exercising those jobs which are the most rewarding in terms of income and social prestige and/or impeding them from acquiring property rights, then the social and economic distributional pattern resulting from the spontaneous order of the market operating under such premises will certainly also reflect these initial discriminations and thus the injustice of the initial configuration of the legal order and the institutions in which market activities are embedded.

The conclusion is that, if we apply the Hayekian understanding of justice as a property of intentional human acts, the distributional outcomes of market processes and the state of affairs created by them can be called 'unjust' and therefore generate a claim to be corrected in the name of justice exactly *insofar as the categories of 'just' and 'unjust' can be applied to the legal and institutional preconditions shaping market outcomes as well as to the persons responsible for the structure of these presuppositions.*[2]

### The limits of Hayek's critique of social justice and the widening of the perspective

It is astonishing that Hayek refrains from further analysis of the possible implications of his statement, cited above, that 'only situations which have been created by human will can be called just or unjust'. In my view this reveals

---

2   Legally held property rights can also be unjust as they have a decisive influence on the framework of market processes, may distort them, and may produce outcomes which can be called unjust – for example, if these 'rights' are acquired by fraud or conquest and illegitimate appropriation, such as of land, and maintained by excluding others from the possibility of acquiring property rights and even work.

what is, despite the essential soundness of his argument against social justice, a clear limitation of his approach.

Hayek fails to consider the possibility that there might exist a higher level of 'rights' and of corresponding 'justice' which could make it plausible to qualify as 'unjust' a determinate state of affairs or distributional patterns resulting from market processes.[3] Although we might agree with Hayek that the distributional outcomes of market processes *as such* cannot be evaluated according to criteria of justice, we still might evaluate these outcomes and the state of affairs created by them on the basis of other, 'higher' or independent criteria which, moreover, *are not criteria of distributional justice* but are much more fundamental and *apply to the legal and institutional framework of society.* Hayek does not provide any argument against such a possibility; he simply does not consider it. Note that I do not intend criticism or modification of the structure of Hayek's verdict against applying the category of justice to the outcomes of market processes. My aim is to show in what way his method and his final verdict on the concept of 'social justice' are incomplete and that, nevertheless, his views on the market can, and need to, be integrated into a wider context of justice.

In order to determine what such criteria of justice might be, I wish to recall the classic definition of justice by the great ancient Roman jurist Ulpian and transmitted through the medieval legal and philosophical tradition,

---

3 Several arguments of this kind have been levelled against Hayek. Some of them are discussed in Tebble (2009). My own argument differs from those discussed by Tebble, however.

especially by Thomas Aquinas, but also referred to spuriously incidentally by Hayek (1976: 154, 165). The definition reads: *Iustitia est constans et perpetua voluntas ius suum cuique tribuendi* (Justice is the constant and perpetual will to render to every man his due).[4]

Once we adopt this classic definition of justice, the question arises whether there is a 'due' (*ius*), that is, 'rights' which human persons as members of society possess *before* they are participants in market processes and independently of their social and economic position – rights which they possess in their capacity as human beings and which therefore do not refer to distributional justice.

The entire Judeo–Christian and subsequent European theological, philosophical, juridical and political tradition is surely, to different degrees, based on this idea. There exists a point of reference of justice, which is human nature: human beings, created in the image of God as free and self-responsible, called to active participation by their proper work, creativity and inventiveness in shaping the world. Most importantly, this initial calling of human beings must not be impeded or frustrated by the legal and institutional framework of society. For this would mean withholding what is 'due' to them, that is, their right, and it would therefore be a violation of justice.

From this derives the idea of 'human rights' in their most fundamental sense: not as necessary legal rights and claims, and certainly not as claims to a determined share in wealth and opportunities, but as moral claims to be

---

4   Ulpian, *Digesta* 1.1.10.

treated as equal qua human beings and with corresponding claims to justice. 'Human rights' are something 'due',
a *ius*, to counteract or despise which is unjust. (For more
detail on this, see Rhonheimer (2011: 282–87).)

Now, in order not to fall into the trap of the concept of
'social justice' as rightly rejected by Hayek, we have to say
that from the existence of such rights we cannot infer that
determinate market outcomes violate these rights and are
therefore unjust. We cannot say this in exactly the same way
as we cannot say that the deaths of human beings caused
by an earthquake are unjust, because an earthquake does
not bring this outcome about intentionally. It is simply a
natural event. We could, however, call the deaths of these
people unjust insofar as they are the consequence of culp-
able and intentional neglect by those responsible for having
fraudulently built poorly designed houses unable to resist a
foreseeable earthquake. Analogously, neither the mere *fact*
of inequality, as caused by market processes, nor the facts
of poverty or lack of opportunity, as states of affairs, can be
considered to be unjust. So far Hayek is right. But he is not
right in denying from the outset that there is no possible
perspective from which market outcomes can be called unjust, in the same way as the deaths of people as a result of
an earthquake could be the consequence of an injustice and
therefore *to that extent* be intentional and unjust.

Consider the case, mentioned earlier, where a legal
and institutional framework of a determinate market
economy is intentionally so designed as to systematically
violate the rights of human beings qua human beings, and
therefore the basic requirements of justice. This injustice is

intentional even if only by voluntary omission: such rights violations take place as a result of not interfering with rather than abolishing a discriminatory framework. In this case, the consequent distortions of market outcomes would be deliberately caused. Therefore, and, insofar as they contradict a valid principle of justice, these distortions could be called unjust to the extent they reflect the injustice of the framework.

So we arrive at two levels of justice. At level one, *the anthropological–foundational level, that of human rights and the corresponding legal and institutional framework of society*, human beings are equal qua human beings, with a shared human nature, and as such they possess dignity. They have a claim on their neighbours to have their dignity respected. We can call these rights 'natural rights' or 'human rights'. In economic life, these rights include the right to actively participate as free and self-responsible beings in shaping the world by their proper work, creativity and inventiveness, thereby obtaining a fair share of the product for their own needs. Violating these rights by impeding their exercise is a breach of justice. And intentionally violating them by means of the general configuration of a society's legal and institutional framework is opposed to what we might still call 'social justice'.

At level two, *the level of the 'catallactic game' of the market*, the outcomes of market processes as such can be qualified neither as just nor as unjust. Yet, as a result of the initial configuration of the legal and institutional framework, these outcomes may be labelled as unjust, not because the market is unjust, but because the initial configuration shaping the market's distributional outcome may violate justice, and transmit this injustice by distorting market outcomes. This presupposes that, even if we conceive of the legal and institutional framework of a market as itself being an order which has evolved spontaneously over time, such an evolution does not exclude human responsibility for the concrete shaping of this order and, thus, indirectly of the distributional outcomes of market processes.

Now, someone could object that to place so much emphasis on human responsibility for the concrete shaping of the legal and institutional framework of a market economy contradicts Hayek's concept of legal order and society as spontaneous orders. But it can be easily shown on Hayekian grounds that there is no such contradiction. Recall that, according to Hayek, the spontaneous order of the evolution of civilisation, society, the legal system and the market economy is not the spontaneity of blind or deterministic natural processes but is always shaped by intentionally acting human beings, by governments, lawyers and legislators whose acts are part of the evolutionary process of such orders (and therefore can turn out better or worse). Thus, Hayek writes regarding the evolution of the legal order, 'the spontaneous process of growth may lead into an impasse from which it cannot extricate itself by its own forces or which it will at least not correct quickly enough' (Hayek 1973: 88). Thus 'a real change in the law is required ... The necessity of such radical changes of particular rules may be due to various causes' such as 'that some past development was based on error or that it produced consequences later *recognized as unjust*' (1973: 89; emphasis added).

According to Hayek, the most frequent cause of the necessity of 'radical changes' in the legal framework is 'that the development of the law has lain in the hands of members of a particular class whose traditional views made them regard as just what could not meet the more general requirements of justice'. He continues: 'There can be no doubt that in such fields as the law of relations between master and servant, landlord and tenant, creditor and debtor, and in modern times between organized business and its customers, *the rules have been shaped largely by the views of one of the parties and their particular interests*' (1973: 89; emphasis added).

These statements demonstrate that Hayek's idea of spontaneous order allows and even requires raising the question of justice regarding precisely those aspects of the economy in which intentional human acts and corresponding responsibility are involved; and this is the level of the legal and institutional preconditions, the basic rules by which markets work. Therefore, the criteria of justice applying to the framing of these legal rules and institutional presuppositions also *indirectly* apply to the outcomes of market processes as far as they are shaped – and possibly distorted – by these legal and institutional preconditions.

For example, it corresponds with human dignity to make a living from one's own work and thereby to acquire through property rights a fair share in the goods of this earth. Now, no market process resulting in winners and losers is morally responsible for the inequality caused by this process. Therefore, categories of justice cannot be applied to them. However, a market process shaped by a discriminatory legal and institutional framework and therefore leading to the exclusion of a determinate group of people from work, keeping them in a state of inescapable poverty and impeding them from becoming property owners, *is a market process distorted by the initial injustice of the legal and institutional framework of society.* Again, it is not the market process itself which can be called unjust; but in this case its outcome reflects an injustice situated at a more fundamental level and which is culpably caused or allowed to continue to exist by intentionally acting human beings.

The principles which can be applied to evaluate these outcomes are not principles of distributional justice situated at the level of the distributional outcome of market processes, but principles located at a higher level, or of a more fundamental kind, referring to human dignity which all human beings have qua human beings and to which they have a corresponding right which is the proper object of the virtue of justice.

In my view this is the sound part of the moral intuition at the root of people's sense of 'social justice' and its corresponding claims. Unfortunately, as a result of fundamental misunderstandings or even ignorance of economics, it has become common to attribute injustice to the free market itself or to 'capitalism', competition, profit-seeking and so on. It is not these, however, that are the problem, but the misperceptions that easily pervert people's sense of justice and thereby generate the notorious 'social justice talk' with its equally notorious call for state intervention, redistribution, and so forth.

Unhappily, it is the sound moral intuition of justice itself that becomes perverted by the unfortunate but popular idea that rich people are rich at the expense of the poor, that their wealth is intentionally withheld or even 'stolen' from the poor. The origin of this is the erroneous belief that the economy is a zero-sum game, that wealth is not continuously *created* anew by those who possess it but is a common asset that is limited such that one person's gain unavoidably means loss or certainly less for other persons, thus impoverishing them.

The perversion of the intuition of social justice can also derive from an egalitarian concept of justice: the idea that inequality *as such* is unjust. This, of course, is equally false. Naturally, mankind is not created equal in every respect; inequality is therefore unavoidable and in practical life it contributes to enrichment by diversification in manifold ways. Moreover, inequality is a consequence of free decisions, of free choice of action, or at least not caused by someone's committing an injustice – provided always that the initial configuration of the legal and institutional framework is not unjust and no fraud or other criminal infraction has been involved in market transactions. Finally, the perversion of the sense of 'social justice' can also be rooted in the conviction – mostly originating in the aforementioned misapprehensions of the nature of the economy and of justice – that society or the state is supposed to compensate the less fortunate or losers in the market process by redistribution, by income transfers and by establishing a welfare state.

To repeat: in my view there is only one legitimate reason to label market outcomes and corresponding inequalities as 'unjust', namely, when the injustice results from the legal and institutional framework that shapes market processes and their outcomes. The fault then is not that of the market, which can be neither just nor unjust. The fault lies in the legal and institutional framework, and those who shaped it or neglected to alter it: human beings such as politicians or citizens are responsible for it, not the market.

Note that I do not contend that market outcomes can be called 'just'. They can be unjust, but only in consequence of an unjust initial legal and institutional framework. Any attempt, on the other hand, at adjusting market outcomes to an alleged pattern of social justice must fail, because we cannot know what the constituent parts of social justice, that is, 'just distribution of income, wealth and opportunities' could be. So, market outcomes are either 'unjust' (in the above-qualified meaning) or, provided the initial framework is just, 'not unjust' or 'not against justice'. This precisely reflects Hayek's insight that, as non-intentional spontaneous orders, market outcomes *as such* cannot be evaluated by criteria of justice. Market outcomes can be unjust only by reference to an unjust configuration of the higher-level framework that *distorts* market outcomes.

These considerations lead us to the following step of the present enquiry into the true meaning of 'social justice'. On the assumption that there is no alternative to the market as the most efficient way for allocating resources, and that it is the only economic order compatible with a free society, the question arises: what are the criteria of justice for the legal and institutional framework of a market economy?

## The social justice of capitalism and of the free market economy

In 1971 the famous American philosopher John Rawls published a book titled *A Theory of Justice*. This book changed not only the academic but also the public discourse on social justice.

Hayek, rather surprisingly perhaps, refers very positively to Rawls's theory of justice, expressing some basic agreement with it (Hayek 1976: 100). However, it seems to me that Hayek was acquainted with Rawls's theory only in a very superficial way. Rawls was a liberal in the popular American sense of the word – a redistributionist social democrat, believing in state welfare provision, state intervention in market outcomes by continuously 'correcting' property distribution, and an educational system driven mainly by the government. Yet one aspect of Rawls's theory is particularly attractive, and this caught Hayek's favourable attention.

Rawls conceived of justice basically as 'fairness'. Justice as fairness means that what justice refers to are the rules, the institutional configurations and procedures which determine socially relevant outcomes. Justice as fairness is based on the assumption that a society is a 'cooperative venture for mutual advantage ' (Rawls 1971: 4) and must therefore be organised in a way which allows to everyone to obtain a fair share of wealth, position, education, social esteem and so on, regardless of his or her initial position in society.

Rawls's theory of justice as fairness is complex and sophisticated. I thus refer to only one feature of it, the so-called difference principle. According to this principle, inequalities are justified only to the extent that they are advantageous also for the less well off. According to Rawls, the basic device for implementing the difference principle is a progressive tax system and, therefore, redistribution of income and property.

As the American libertarian political scientist and philosopher John Tomasi argues in his book *Free Market Fairness*, Rawls's theory of justice and particularly the difference principle is based on the sound assumption that an economic system should be advantageous for everybody; otherwise it would be unfair. He calls this the 'distributional adequacy condition' (Tomasi 2012: 126). An economic order that, as such and on principle, undermines the position of the most disadvantaged, creating wealth and inequality at the expense of the least advantaged and generally of those who are less well off, would not meet the distributional adequacy condition and therefore would be unfair and unjust.

Tomasi shows that, for a wide range of classical liberals from Adam Smith to Ronald Reagan, this assumption that capitalism and a free market economy are most beneficial *for everybody*, including the poor, was always a decisive consideration in their *moral* justification. According to Tomasi, Hayek is no exception (2012: 136). Here Tomasi argues that a Hayekian view better fulfils the criterion of the distributional adequacy condition than does Rawls's theory of justice. Certainly, for Hayek the fundamental rationale for a market economy is that only the market order is compatible with liberty and a free society in which everybody can act according to his or her own knowledge and preferences. Hayek is convinced, however, that for exactly this reason – the primacy of liberty – everyone, including the least advantaged, is given a chance. This is why it is legitimate on Hayekian grounds to call such an order 'fair' or 'just'. Note that in this case the qualification 'just' does not refer to the outcome or the market process, but to the legal and institutional initial framework shaping the outcome of market processes.

Let us, therefore – at least for the sake of argument – assume that on a most abstract level Rawls's difference principle is correct. That is, let us assume that the initial legal and institutional configuration of the economic order must be such that existing or growing inequality is advantageous for all, not excluding the poorest social groups; and that a framing of the basic structure of this kind corresponds to justice so that the outcomes of market processes shaped by it, whatever they are, cannot be called 'unjust' or need to be corrected in the name of justice.

I have mentioned Rawls's contention that the distributional adequacy condition – the difference principle – is best met in a property-owning democracy in which incomes are redistributed by a progressive tax system, even if redistribution implies the slowing down of economic growth. Now, another political philosopher, Jason Brennan, also cited by Tomasi, has shown that this position is self-defeating. Brennan calls this 'Rawls' paradox' (Brennan 2007). The paradox is that the requirements of the difference principle and thus of the distributional adequacy condition are far better met in a society with a completely free market that completely abstains from redistributionist policies and instead gives absolute priority to economic efficiency, that is, the capitalist dynamics of economic growth. But if this is the case, under Rawls's difference principle such a society would also have to be called more just.

Brennan demonstrates this theoretically using a thought experiment comparing two fictitious societies, called respectively 'ParetoSuperiorland' and 'Fairnessland'. The two societies have the same starting conditions. But while ParetoSuperiorland focuses only on economic efficiency, giving absolute priority to growth, Fairnessland, under the influence of Rawls's conception of justice, starts redistributing income and wealth according to a fixed pattern of distribution considered to be fair. This requires that its government interfere with the market's spontaneous allocations of resources, and thus it retards growth. 'Such interference entails interrupting the information, incentive and learning structure of the market, thus disrupting the operation of the equilibrium principles that generate efficiency and growth. Rawls has granted us all of this – these are his premises' (Brennan 2007: 293).

Brennan points that, with the power of compound growth rates, after a generation the poorest in Pareto-Superiorland are much better off in money terms than the poorest in Fairnessland. Brennan not only argues on the basis of this thought model but also makes an empirical case. He admits: 'It certainly is true that growth does not guarantee a benefit to the poor – it is even compatible with harming them. However, historically, when growth harms the poor, *it is usually because property rights regimes and the rule of law are not in place*' (2007: 294; emphasis added). This refers precisely to the initial configuration of the legal and institutional framework of an economy on which discourses about social justice should be focused. Cultural factors may also play a role in making market outcomes harm the poorest, like the Indian caste system (but such factors might also be described, at least according to Western standards, as contributing to a deficient property rights regime and unjust derogations from the 'rule of law').

We arrive at the conclusion that, *in the long run* and from a strictly economic point of view, and in the presence of a just initial legal and institutional configuration including the rule of law and the assurance of property rights for all without discrimination, the increased inequality resulting from capital accumulation is much more effective in enriching the poor than is redistribution. So, according to the difference principle, it would also be more just. Especially from the standpoint of future generations, 'social justice' seems be on the side of an unfettered free market economy and against any kind of redistribution with the aim of reducing inequality.

The only reason to consider redistribution superior would be a focus – albeit at some expense to future generations – on the short-term improvement of the situation of determinate social groups of poor and disadvantaged people. This again has the same aim as Hayek when he advocates 'an insurance against extreme misfortune' (1976: 87). This might be a public relief programme for the poor, preferably organised by local communities: not a redistributive policy to remodel society by permanently reducing inequality,[5] but rather part of a public service for those in need.

Note that even short-term advantages for the poorest in consequence of redistributive policies do not necessarily provide real improvement for them. It may be an improvement in current money income, but not necessarily in their opportunities. Real prosperity, wealth and the enhancement of opportunities are created by a rise in productivity, which is the consequence of both capital accumulation and technological innovation. As Jason Brennan rightly emphasises: 'The biggest predictor and cause of increases in worker quality of life is capital accumulation, since this drives up the productivity of labor, and labor prices' (Brennan 2007: 294). And this is the point of the whole story. People in ParetoSuperiorland will not be wealthier simply in the sense of *money income*. They will be better off in every respect: they will be more productive, that is, they will have higher levels of skill and education and therefore of opportunities; the society they live in will be technologically more advanced, which also signifies that more of those goods which previously were luxury goods available only to members of the highest-income class will now be available for mass consumption, including by the poorest. So, even if – because of inevitable capital accumulation – in terms of wealth and money income as reflected in

---

5   Note that by contrast the French economist Thomas Piketty (2013) argues for a reduction in inequality (by confiscatory levels of taxation) not so much to help the poor as to reduce inequality per se, which he considers unjust and socially disruptive.

statistics the gap between the richest and the poorest will increase, in terms of the *real standard of living* – including education and opportunities – the gap will simultaneously dramatically decrease. We can recognise that exactly this is what has already happened when we compare the gap between everyday living standards, in terms of household appliances, health care, available information technology, means of transportation, education and so forth, of people like Bill Gates and those of present-day blue-collar workers with the gap between the everyday living standards of the very rich in the nineteenth century – say a John Rockefeller or an Andrew Carnegie – and those of an average factory worker at that time. Not even the richest king in the past enjoyed the standard of living which capitalist growth and its technologically innovative power has provided to each citizen in modern societies.

Given the unquestionable efficiency of capitalism and a free market in raising prosperity for all, the real question of 'social justice' therefore seems to be the question of the fairness or justice of the initial configuration of the legal and institutional framework making possible this efficiency and giving everybody without discrimination a fair chance of sharing in its fruits. Once it is acknowledged that markets are best in allocating resources efficiently (which Rawls does not deny), and redistribution is ruled out as the best way of meeting the distributional adequacy condition – or the difference principle – we only have to establish the criteria for a fair and just initial legal and institutional framework of a market order which guarantees the respect of the basic human rights of every single person without discrimination. It is clear that, *as far as politics and public institution building is concerned*, the term 'social justice' can have a meaning only in terms of this framework.

This question obviously has nothing to do with questions of material equality or even equality of opportunities as they exist at the beginning of the process; it concerns, rather, solely *the rules governing the market process*. These are relatively easy to identify. Besides normal provisions of penal law against theft, homicide, fraud and so forth and the regulation of contracts (i.e. the rule of law), they essentially comprise securing of property rights and the public services needed to enforce them (e.g. land registers). It must be warranted by law that nobody is excluded from acquiring such rights and that possible bureaucratic or other impediments to doing so are abolished. The legal system and institutions must be such that any person, without discrimination of any kind, can make a living from working, whatever form this might take, whether by starting and managing one's own business or as an employee.

At the level of constitutional law, the legal system must furthermore make sure that no economic interest and no group in the market receives any legal privilege in the form of monopoly rights, subsidies or other kinds of favour. Any collusion between those holding political power and the players of the 'catallactic game' of the market (i.e. business-people, entrepreneurs, bankers, investors, employees and so on) must be banned by law, while freedom of contract in the labour marked must be assured.

This amounts to saying that a basically just order exists when a capitalist market economy is founded on a legal and institutional framework that guarantees the rule of law and a fair regime of property rights, and refrains from redistribution with the aim of correcting the distributional outcomes of the market process. Where this is the case, we can say that it corresponds to social justice because we are talking about the justice of the rules that shape society and not the distributional effects of market outcomes.

From yet another, very important, point of view, such an order is again in accordance with social justice: a capitalist market economy which refrains from redistributing income for reasons of social justice also implies that human dignity and the claims and rights deriving from it are respected on the basis of *multiple sources*. For example, in the labour market a just wage is the wage which corresponds to a worker's productivity and to the contractual obligations freely accepted by the parties to a labour contract. Now, because of a worker's low levels of education, skill or productivity, such a wage might not suffice to provide a living. Nevertheless, this is no reason to hold that the *employer* – who already pays for the value of work done – should also be responsible for covering the rest by the additional payment of a 'family wage' or 'living wage'. There is no *moral* reason for setting up legal minimum wages (and many good economic and social reasons, too, against it), no *moral* basis for demanding, as a requirement of social justice, the redistribution of some of the income of the richest to supplement workers' insufficient wages. (In any case, this would also be economically harmful and decrease general prosperity by providing wrong incentives.)

It is exactly at his point, however, that the perspective of social justice starts to become even wider. Social justice does not merely refer to institutional configurations and state regulations, it does not relate only to politics and public institution building, but is to be understood in a much broader way. Basically, it is human persons who are just or unjust. Therefore, social justice also is something attributable not only to the legal and institutional framework of society but also, *and even in the first place*, to freely and intentionally acting human beings (who, after all, are also the ones responsible for the concrete shaping of the legal and institutional framework, which is precisely why it may be unjust). The concept of social justice applied to human actions refers to the quality of their bearing upon the overall condition of society – the rights, opportunities and legitimate needs of its members – that is, upon the common good.

Moreover, there is not only the *labour* market. There exist also markets for social and health services, for education, for insurance against any kind of misfortune, which call into play entrepreneurial initiative. Although, *or even exactly because*, they are profit-oriented, such entrepreneurial initiative and creativity are necessarily oriented towards satisfying the determined needs and preferences of consumers (including the consumers of health provision, education, insurance, old-age provision and so forth). Otherwise no profit could be possibly made by such entrepreneurial activities. But because there may be needs which cannot be satisfied by profit-seeking entrepreneurial activity, there remains the wide field of non-profit and voluntary and charitable organisations which help to meet the determined needs especially of the poorest, and which form a privileged field for exercising social justice as a *virtue*. All of this is part of the realisation of social justice in the sense of respecting the dignity of humans as free and responsible beings created in the image of God and their corresponding rights. It is social justice which becomes solidarity and is perfected by charity.

Such things are completely overlooked if social justice and human rights are seen only in the context of claims against the state, calling for redistributionist policies which not only are detrimental to the increase of general prosperity but are also morally questionable because they are based on compulsory taxation and therefore a state invasion into the property rights of precisely those citizens who most contribute to economic growth and thus to general prosperity. This has nothing to do with justice, but rather with unjust confiscation which, being moreover economically harmful, is opposed to the common good and therefore to social justice.

With these remarks we have approached a dimension of social justice which is worlds away from current social justice talk. It is, however, rather close to a way of understanding social justice in the Catholic tradition, to which I now turn.

## Social justice in Catholic social doctrine

The very term 'social justice' was most probably first used by the Italian Jesuit and philosopher Luigi Taparelli d'Azeglio.

For him, social justice was simply 'justice between man and man', which consisted of respecting in every human being *i diritti di umanità*, 'the rights of humanity'. This corresponds to what I have attributed above to level one. Moreover, Taparelli d'Azeglio (1883: 152) emphasised that a part of social justice is also to respect the natural inequalities between human beings which are relevant not to their belonging to the human species, but to their place and role in society, such as the difference between a father and a son.

Of course, this has nothing to do with our contemporary concept of 'social justice' as an alleged kind of distributive justice. But it is the way the term was invented and then propagated by the nineteenth-century Catholic priest and philosopher Antonio Rosmini in 1848 (Rosmini 2007). Only later was the term 'social justice' assumed by the German school of solidarism founded by the Jesuit economist and social philosopher Heinrich Pesch, a school in which Gustav Gundlach and Oswald von Nell-Breuning (also Jesuits), the drafters of the encyclical *Quadragesimo anno*, had been nurtured. Like the principle of subsidiarity, the term 'social justice' was introduced into the common vocabulary by this encyclical, issued by Pope Pius XI on 15 May 1931.[6] *Quadragesimo anno* used it in a peculiar way, maintaining that competition was not sufficient as a principle to regulate the economy; it needed, so the encyclical says, to be complemented by 'social justice' and 'social love'. According to Nell-Breuning's well-known extensive

---

6   http://www.vatican.va/holy_father/pius_xi/encyclicals/documents/hf_p
-xi_enc_19310515_quadragesimo-anno_en.html

commentary on the encyclical, 'social justice' referred to the state and its task to establish a legal and institutional order on the basis of which the market could operate for the common good (Nell-Breuning 1932: 169–71). There was no mention of correcting market outcomes by redistribution. Rather, social justice was seen as a supreme regulatory framework established by state authority with a view to channelling market competition according to a principle of order.

This is certainly a use of the term 'social justice' that could be understood in the sense I have elaborated so far. It is interesting that a neoliberal economist like Wilhelm Röpke praised the view of *Quadragesimo anno* as exactly corresponding to his own ordoliberal view of a free market economy embedded in a framework of rules assuring that it is not corrupted by monopolies and cartels (Röpke 1944: 18). However, social justice as mentioned in *Quadragesimo anno* refers to the *state* – that is, according to Nell-Breuning, to the idea that the state is ultimately responsible for the good functioning of a market economy. This assumption is based on the belief that the market cannot regulate itself so that it promotes the common good. Therefore, the idea of social justice as it appears in *Quadragesimo anno* contains a bias: it readily leads to a mentality which in the end calls for state intervention in order to 'correct' the market and its outcomes in the name of 'social justice'.[7]

---

7   A basic problem of *Quadragesimo anno* is its misinterpretation of the causes of the 1929 crash and the subsequent economic depression. The encyclical mentions the problem of the financial and especially the credit system as a main cause, which is certainly correct, but it attributes its

Understood in this sense, the older meaning of the term has given way to a more political understanding focusing on the role of the state. This more political meaning is also the meaning of social justice that the *Catechism of the Catholic Church* Nr. 1928 suggests: 'Society ensures social justice when it provides the conditions that allow associations or individuals to obtain what is their due, according to their nature and their vocation. Social justice is linked to the common good and the exercise of authority.' Accordingly, social justice – ensured by 'society' and 'linked to the common good and the exercise of authority' – appears to lie essentially, or at least predominantly, within the state's sphere of responsibility.[8]

The statement obviously includes the assumption that only state authority is capable of guaranteeing that the different social forces and individual actions contribute to the common good.[9] It thus opens the way to all sorts of in-

---

malfunctioning to the forces of market competition. In reality, the cause was – besides the catastrophic macroeconomic disequilibria caused by the provisions of the Treaty of Versailles of 1919 – the monetary system which during the 'roaring twenties' stimulated an enormous credit expansion causing large-scale malinvestment and a boom which was not sustainable. All the policies meant to combat the following bust were based on state intervention and in fact aggravated the problem precisely because they prevented market forces from making the necessary adjustments (which for a shorter period would have certainly been very painful).

8   Nr. 1929–1942 mentions several aspects of social justice, referring to it as a moral virtue exercised by individual human persons. (The part of the *Catechism of the Catholic Church* that deals with social justice is available at https://www.vatican.va/archive/ENG0015/__P6N.HTM.)

9   For a more detailed critique of this idea still prevalent in modern Catholic social teaching, especially since the encyclical *Pacem in terris* of 1963 by John XXIII, see Rhonheimer (2013).

terpretations in terms of economic policies. In the name of 'social justice', Catholic social teaching favours, according to the *Compendium of the Social Doctrine of the Church* published in 2004 by the Pontifical Council for Justice and Peace at the request of John Paul II, 'social policies for the redistribution of income which, taking general conditions into account, look at merit as well as at the need of each citizen'. The rationale given for this is that the measure of just income should be 'the objective value of the work rendered' as well as 'the human dignity of the subjects who perform it' (Nr. 303).[10]

It seems to me that this confuses the two levels of justice mentioned on page 172. It pretends to meet the requirements of human dignity (level one) by correcting market outcomes with redistributive policies or by even interfering with market mechanisms (which concerns level two), without any consideration, however, of the origin of the violation of dignity in the configuration of the legal and institutional framework itself (which pertains to our level two). Like Rawls's theory of justice, such teaching does not take into account, or even mention, the relationship between economic growth and the rise in productivity and general prosperity on the one hand, and the harmful social and economic consequences of redistributive politics in the name of 'social justice' on the other.

---

10 The official English translation of the *Compendium of the Social Doctrine of the Church* is available at http://www.vatican.va/roman_curia/pontifi cal_councils/justpeace/documents/rc_pc_justpeace_doc_20060526 _compendio-dott-soc_en.html.

Redistributive policies are not directed to the *common good* but only to the short-term good of particular social groups – unfortunately and typically, of the constituencies of politicians whose concern is being elected or re-elected. Moreover, it is a serious threat to a free society when the 'needs' and 'merits' of its members, as the *Compendium* suggests, are to be evaluated by politicians and state bureaucracies, and benefits distributed accordingly. In addition, this opens the way to the corruption as well as the perversion of democracy, by constituency-driven political promises that inevitably cause ever-increasing public indebtedness.

The *Compendium* thus commits a very frequent error which is characteristic also of Rawls's *Theory of Justice* and many similar philosophical theories of justice: it argues on the level of ideal moral reasoning in disregard of real-world conditions and basic economic facts concerning the creation of wealth and the way in which legal and economic measures effectively improve the condition of the poorest. This is why I cannot consider its recommendations helpful for promoting the common good, that is, the overall good in the long run and for all people living in a given society, including the generations to come.[11] Redistributionist

---

11 Notice that the definition of the term 'common good' in *Catechism* Nr. 1906, quoting *Gaudium et spes*, one of the key pastoral documents resulting from the Second Vatican Council and promulgated by Pope Paul VI in 1965, also applies to what I have just said: 'By common good is to be understood "the sum total of social conditions which allow people, either as groups or as individuals, to reach their fulfilment more fully and more easily".' The common good to be pursued at a given time refers to all, and also to future generations.

social policies serve only particular groups of people, only in the short run and at the expense of the general prosperity of present as well as future generations, too: at the expense, that is, precisely of the common good.

Apart from the required justice of the legal and institutional framework of society in general and of the market in particular – to create and uphold which is the task of state authority – the realisation of 'social justice' should be primarily placed in the hands of individual persons acting alone or as entrepreneurs in all kinds of private associations. This corresponds with a more basic meaning of 'social justice' typical of an older tradition and also mentioned, briefly but not very clearly, in Nr. 202 of the *Compendium*. According to this tradition, 'social justice' essentially is what justice generally is: a moral virtue of human persons and not a measure of 'just distribution' of wealth and income. In this older sense, 'social justice' is identified with what Thomas Aquinas called 'general justice' and what later has been also called 'legal justice' (on this see Gregg 2013a, 2013b: 173–75). General or legal justice is the justice of individual persons in their actions as far as these actions refer not to the good of a single person but to the common good. In this sense, Antonio Rosmini wrote in *La società e il suo fine* (1837): 'public good must be sought in the private citizen; social justice in individual justice. The foundation stone of the social edifice must be virtue, buried deep in the human heart' (Rosmini 1994: 119).

The object of the virtue of justice is the 'due', which is the *ius*, the right of each person. A capitalist who invests his wealth, or part of it, in growth-producing entrepreneurial activity creating workplaces, or an entrepreneur who seeks to make a profit by satisfying consumer needs, thus contributes to technological innovation, to increased productivity and in consequence to a rise in real wages and general prosperity also for generations to come. They contribute more to the common good than any state policy redistributing income and thereby slowing down economic growth and the rise in general prosperity. This, in my view, is what economics teaches and what has to be taken into account when one talks about 'social justice'. Precisely insofar as 'social justice' means the virtue of general or legal justice, the profitable activity of capitalists and entrepreneurs in the free market contributes more to social justice, to the common good, than anything the state can do – except the task of assuring the legal and institutional framework, mainly the regime of property rights which is the *state's* specific and indispensable contribution to the common good.

Social justice as a virtue leads to understanding how important it is that all citizens feel responsible for the common good, that they can't simply delegate this duty of justice and solidarity to the state. And according to the principle of subsidiarity cherished by Catholic social doctrine, they *should not* delegate it to the state. Subsidiarity, however, does not mean that the state leaves only less important tasks to society while it concentrates on the most important ones, but that it helps and assists the 'lower' communities and individuals to fulfil their tasks, without assuming them itself. This is how the principle was defined in Nr. 48 of the encyclical *Centesimus annus*, an encyclical written by Pope John Paul II in 1991: 'a community of a higher order should not interfere in the internal life of a community of a lower order, depriving the latter of its functions, but rather should support it in case of need and help to coordinate its activity with the activities of the rest of society, always with a view to the common good.' This, according to Nr. 15 of *Centesimus annus*, is also applied to the market economy: 'Indirectly and according to the *principle of subsidiarity*' the state creates 'favourable conditions for the free exercise of economic activity, which will lead to abundant opportunities for employment and sources of wealth'. This, and not redistribution of income to reduce inequality, is the state's fundamental contribution to the common good and to social justice.[12]

## Conclusion

To conclude: the concept of 'social justice' need not be entirely rejected or even relegated to the category of 'nonsense', as Hayek claims (1976: 78). It is, however, a very insidious term and nowadays mostly used in a vague and emotional way often detrimental to the common good. But

12 Admittedly, in the following sentence *Centesimus annus* states: 'Directly and according to the *principle of solidarity* [the State must contribute] by defending the weakest, by placing certain limits on the autonomy of the parties who determine working conditions, and by ensuring in every case the necessary minimum support for the unemployed worker.' Such recommendations can be counterproductive and again it is entirely disputable whether state intervention is the right way to attain these goals. (The text of *Centesimus annus* is available at http://www.vatican.va/holy_father/john _paul_ii/encyclicals/documents/hf_jp-ii_enc_01051991_centesimus-an nus_en.html.)

there is what we might call a 'true meaning' of social justice. It derives from the higher level of considering human
dignity as derived from human nature, and the rights
springing from that dignity. Taking this into account, we
can apply the category of justice to the basic legal and
institutional framework of a society, and, regarding the
economy, of the free market (mainly the rule of law and
a regime of property rights). It makes sense to talk about
'social justice' regarding the fairness of this framework, especially with reference to the justice of the persons responsible for the concrete shaping of this framework, *which in
fact is the basic common good of human society.*[13] As social
justice is essentially a moral virtue, it also applies to all
other actions of human beings insofar as they relate to the
common good. Social justice in this sense applies to the
actions of capitalists, investors and entrepreneurs, and
also to citizens feeling responsible for persons in need and
for the poor (which should apply especially to Christians).[14]

---

13  See Benedict XVI, encyclical *Caritas in veritate* of 2009, Nr. 7: 'To take a
    stand for the common good is on the one hand to be solicitous for, and on
    the other hand to avail oneself of, that complex of institutions that give [sic]
    structure to the life of society, juridically, civilly, politically and culturally,
    making it the *pólis*, or "city" ... This is the institutional path – we might
    also call it the political path – of charity, no less excellent and effective
    than the kind of charity which encounters the neighbour directly, outside
    the institutional mediation of the *pólis.*' Available at http://www.vatican
    .va/holy_father/benedict_xvi/encyclicals/documents/hf_ben-xvi_enc_20
    090629_caritas-in-veritate_en.html.

14  As far as Christians are concerned, we have to keep in mind that the fam-
    ous 'preferential option for the poor' is an option *of the Church.* It cannot be
    a *preferential* option of the market or the state, because these are called to
    serve the common good and not the good of the poor alone. Here lies one of
    the roots of ecclesiastical and clerical confusion: applying the theological

As it seems to me, Catholic social teaching still suffers from a prejudice against the socially beneficial nature of freedom. It therefore mistrusts market mechanisms and places too much confidence in the state as a promoter of the common good, completely disregarding the terrible dangers of the abuse of power and of government failure. Being focused too much on moral argument and ideal theory, thereby disregarding the logic of economic thinking, it still does not sufficiently appreciate that it is precisely the spontaneous order of the market that promotes the common good and thus social justice much better than any attempt by means of the state and its bureaucracies to shape society according to a pattern of alleged 'social justice'.

principle of the preferential option for the poor to the realm of politics and the economy. This is a fundamental category error. Theological principles of mercy, gift and charity cannot and must not be applied to economics and politics. The preferential option for the poor is an option specific to the activity of the Church.

# 9 THE LIBERTARIAN CHARACTER OF THE ISLAMIC ECONOMY

Ali Salman

## Glossary of Islamic terms

*fiqh*   Islamic jurisprudence largely developed by four leading jurists in the first two centuries after the death of the Prophet Muhammad in 632 AD

*hadith* (pl. *ahadith*)   Sayings of the Prophet Muhammad

*hijra(t)*   Migration of the Prophet Muhammad from Mecca to Medina

*hisba*   Business accountability

*mu'akhat*   The arrangement of sharing of properties between the Muslims migrating from Mecca and host Muslims from Medina upon *hijrat*

*mutsahib*   A supervisor of bazaars and trade in the medieval Islamic countries

*najsh*   Artificial bidding up the price by a third party without an intention to buy it (literally: 'he concealed himself')

*sahaba*   Companions of the Prophet Muhammad, who embraced Islam in his life and met him

*shari'a*   Islamic divine law derived from primary sources (*Quran, sunnah* and *hadith*)

*sunnah*   Practice by the Prophet Muhammad

*tas'ir*   Price control

Islam is not just the world's fastest-growing religion, governing more than a billion lives; it is also the most potent political currency in the world's economically most strategic areas. Prosperity and peace in these areas depends largely on the degree of legitimacy that free market economics would enjoy in an increasingly reactionary ideological environment underpinned by specific religious interpretations. Seen in this way, the question of the compatibility of free market economics with Islam has global implications.

This chapter discusses the compatibility of free market economics with *shari'a* by juxtaposing literature from the *Quran, hadith* and *fiqh* against the arguments of certain twentieth-century Islamic economists and scholars. Unlike most modern treatments of Islamic economics, this essay does not seek to compare and contrast Islamic law with prevalent discourses on economics that have resulted in 'Islamic capitalism' or 'Islamic socialism'. Rather, it revisits the intellectual tensions within Islamic discourse by discussing the ideas of economic freedom and social justice, and aims to show that, at least in the domain of economics, the goal of justice is largely achieved by ensuring freedom.

The chapter suggests that it is important to rediscover the economic insights offered in the earlier Islamic texts, but not in search of some pure type of economic system, for no such system exists. Rather, the quest should be for an historical understanding of certain intellectual positions that draw their authority from Islam and continue to influence the domain of public policy in Islamic countries.

Such analysis is especially important in relation to countries like Pakistan, whose constitution is officially subject to the boundaries prescribed by *shari'a*.

The next section of this chapter presents the basic principles of economics found in the primary sources of *shari'a*, namely the *Quran* and *hadith*. The following section presents the key arguments of certain twentieth-century Islamic economists on the issues of economic freedom, welfare and social justice. The concluding section restates the salient characteristics of Islamic economic philosophy.

## The principles of economics in Islam

This section presents the important principles and features of economics in Islam derived from the *Quran*, *hadith* and *fiqh*. Admittedly, what follows by way of evidence will be selective, but it is hoped that the primary nature of these verdicts, being based directly on the *Quran* and *hadith*, will help in substantiating the argument. As this discussion shows, the economic system of an Islamic state ought to be based on the principles of freedom, mutual consent and exchange. In terms of policy, this leads to the affirmation of private property rights, the absence of price controls and the endorsement of a risk–return conceptualisation of wealth creation.

### *Voluntary exchange*

The fundamental principle of economic transactions is captured in the following Quranic verse, which enjoins its followers to observe voluntary exchange and thrift (4: 29; Dawood 1999):

> Believers, do not consume your wealth among yourselves in vanity, but rather trade with it by mutual consent.

Another leading translator and interpreter of the *Quran*, Abdullah Yusuf Ali, has translated the same verse thus (4: 29; Ali 1934: 53):

> O ye who believe! Eat up not your property among yourselves in vanities; but let there be amongst you traffic and trade by mutual good-will.

Commenting on this verse, Ali writes, 'Here it occurs to encourage us to increase property by economic use (traffic and trade) recalling Christ's parable of the talents (Matt. 25: 14–30), where the servants who had increased their master's wealth were promoted and the servant who hoarded was cast into darkness' (Ali 1934: 54). This verse should form the ethical and moral foundations of the economic policy of an Islamic state as it combines the basic sources of prosperity, namely, property, thrift and exchange.

## *Acceptance of inequality as a divine scheme*

The *Quran* enjoins its followers to accept socio-economic inequality as a part of the divine scheme. Thus, inequality in its own right may not be construed as tantamount to an injustice. The *Quran* is explicit on this point at several places, for instance (43: 32):

It is we who deal out to them their livelihood in this world, exalting some in rank above others, so that one may take the other into his service.

Commenting on this verse, Abdullah Yusuf Ali (1934: 347) writes, 'In his wisdom, God allows some to grow in power or riches, and command work for others, and various relative gradations are established'. It shows that in terms of socio-economic status, Islam not only condones inequality but attributes it to a divine scheme.

## Sanctity of property rights

The sanctity of private property rights is derived from extensive Quranic injunctions on inheritance and charity, mentioned on a number of occasions. Although this remains an inference, a more direct verdict in favour of protection of private property can be found in the last sermon of the Prophet, which he began with these words:

O People, just as you regard this month, this day, this city as sacred, so regard the life and property of every Muslim as a sacred trust.

## Free trade

The Prophet of Islam, himself having led the life of an active trader for 40 years, had permitted trade even with the enemy. In a state document issued during the time of the Prophet, the Prophet issued a writ of protection from 'God and Muhammad' in favour of Yuhannah ibn R'bah and the people of Ailah, for trade via sea and land. It should be noted that before that writ was issued the said tribes and their lands had been subdued and annexed by the Prophet (Yusuf 1990).

## Price control

The issue of *tas'ir* (price control by the state) has exercised Islamic jurists for centuries. The *Quran* is silent on it, and we are therefore left with *hadith* – the traditions of the Prophet Muhammad – as a benchmark for understanding religious notions about price control within the Islamic framework. According to a tradition of the Prophet, *tas'ir* is forbidden, as it is an injustice and as prices are determined by God. Various *ahadith* convey the same meaning and message, and are recorded in all leading compilations of *ahadith* except *Sahih Bukhari*. According to a *hadith* (*Al-Tirmidhi* on the authority of Anas ibn Malik):

> At the time of the Messenger of God, the market price rose in Medina. The people said, 'O Messenger of God, fix the price'. He replied, 'God is the taker and the disposer, the provider, and the controller of prices. I hope that when I meet Him none of you will have a claim against me for an injury concerning life and property'.

There is a general consensus among the four leading schools of thought in the *fiqh* of the *sunni* Islamic tradition to the effect that price control is proscribed in Islam, although some interpretations have sanctioned intervention in order to protect consumers. The *shi'a* tradition also legitimises the prohibition on state intervention in price setting, although the *hadith* narrated in *shi'a* literature is different. Accordingly, when the price of goods fluctuated considerably, the Prophet was requested to set a price. The Prophet reportedly said (Va'ezzadeh Khorasani, quoted in Nomani and Rehnema 1994: 58):

> I will not set such a precedent, let the people carry on with their activities and benefit mutually; if, however, you wish to give them advice, that will not be objectionable.

Islamic jurists had clearly understood the consequences of price control. Imam Shamsuddeen Ibn Qudamah al-Maqdidi (d. 1304 AD), a Hanbali jurist, argued against any kind of state intervention in the market. He wrote (Ibn Qudamah, quoted in Bashar 1997: 32):

> In a way the control of price may give rise to price rise. The traders from outside will not bring their goods in a place where they would be forced to sell them at a price against their wish. The local traders would hide the goods instead of selling. People would have less than their need, so they would offer a higher price to obtain the goods. Both parties (sellers and buyers) would lose; the sellers because they were prevented from selling their goods, and the buyers because there were prevented from fulfilling their needs. So this act will be termed as forbidden.

Ibn Qudamah clearly understood two harmful effects of price control: the emergence of black markets, and unsatisfied consumer needs. Thus, for this school consideration of the needs of both sellers and buyers shows that price control reduces welfare.

## Profit and wealth creation

A market price always contains a profit margin for the seller; and it is an established tenet of commerce that higher risk entails higher profit. What constitutes profit? A very comprehensive *hadith* identifies the crux of profit in these terms (Sunan Abi Dawood, quoted by Usmani 2010; author's translation):

> Profit earned depends on the degree of risk assumed.

This implies that Islamic law does not define any quantitative upper limit on the degree of profit to be earned, but ties it to the degree of risk assumed. Of course, in a competitive economy any trader taking extraordinary profits in commodity markets would soon find new suppliers offering the same goods at a lower price.

## Muhtasib: Consumer protection and enforcement of contracts

The early Islamic state saw the appointment of an officer, *muhtasib*, or the organisation of *hisba* (business accountability), in the city markets, largely for the purpose of inspection and regulation. The first *muhtasib* in Islamic history was Umar, one of the most trusted companions of the Prophet and the second Caliph of Islam, who was appointed by the Prophet himself. Essentially, the Prophet delegated the tasks of visiting the markets for the purpose of inspection and weight measurements to Umar. However, as established, price fixing was beyond the jurisdiction of the *muhtasib* (Dost 2009). Later, another noted Islamic scholar, Al-Mawardi, elaborated the duties of the *muhtasib*. For him, 'the market supervisor (*muhtasib*) is simply a coordinator of marketplace on the principles of "enjoining the right and forbidding the wrong"'.[1] His functions pertaining to the economic realm included inspecting measures, the quality of products, and the integrity of contracts in the market (Dost 2009). His other duties included dealing with 'market rigidities such as *bay al-gharar* (speculative sales), *najsh*, price discrimination, monopolistic practices, collusion, dumping, hoarding of necessities and others' (Oran 2010: 134). A *muhtasib* was authorised to give advice, issue reprimands, obstruct by force, threaten, imprison or even expel individuals from the market.

## *Economic freedom and the concept of welfare in Islam*

The foregoing discussion establishes that Islam ordains an environment of economic freedom with minimum state

---

1   To translate *ma'ruf* and *munkar* as 'right' and 'wrong' makes them relative. The original sense of *ma'ruf* is *'urf*, 'practice' or 'norm' (Muhammad Khalid Masud, email conversation, 4 May 2012).

intervention. In principle, economic freedom is guaranteed and there is a strong rationale for believing that it is the economic freedom of both buyers and sellers that constitutes the central pillar of Islamic economic policy. The natural question that arises is that, if this conclusion is accepted, then what does Islam offer to the weak and the poor? How can a regime that is supposedly non-interventionist by design fulfil its obligations towards those of its citizens who are poor, excluded or marginalised?

It is argued that the welfare that forms the central concern of an Islamic state comes not from controls and distribution but from liberty, enterprise and charity. As the introduction of *hisba* suggests, the Islamic state ensures consumer protection from theft, fraud or coercion through both legal and moral obligations. Thus, the protective aspect of an Islamic state is essentially focused on ensuring the absence of harm rather than the provision or redistribution of goods; it is negative rather than positive.

Thus, the economic policy of *shari'a* can arguably be understood as a validation of the notion of negative freedom. The concepts of negative and positive freedom were articulated by Isaiah Berlin (1958). Negative freedom means freedom from coercion, whereas positive freedom means freedom to act. J. S. Mill (1859) and F. A. Hayek (1960) advocated negative freedom as a principle of public policy. It was argued that if the state could protect its citizens from coercion in any form, and from any party, it almost guaranteed their welfare without directly providing for it.

There is no doubt that Islam calls for compassion towards others, but this call is essentially moral and voluntary in nature; otherwise, the example of *mu'akhat* set by the Prophet and his worthy companions upon *hijrat*, wherein the Muslims of Medina shared and gave up half of their property to their brethren migrating from Mecca, would have been codified into a law, which would have prescribed that any surplus property owned by a Muslim should be given to a needy brother or neighbour. But this brotherhood remains voluntary in nature, and is not legally enforceable. The forcible appropriation of property is by general consensus regarded an injustice, a *zulm*. So the notion of forced redistribution seems alien to Islamic law and the spirit of its injunctions.

In summary, the institutional proscription of price control and the ensuring of consumer protection at the same time constitute the two most important elements of the Islamic market. It may be inferred that the letter of *shari'a* calls for economic freedom but its attendant systems of consumer protection and free and fair competition provide the foundation of social justice. Seen this way, Islam provides its followers with a firm moral foundation for economic transactions.

## Islamic economics: signposts to statism

This section reviews some of most important topics that are generally debated in Islamic economics. It revisits the arguments of certain leading Islamic economists of the twentieth century,[2] such as Nejatullah Siddiqi, Syed Nawab

---

2   While the tradition of applying Islamic principles to trade and finance is as old as Islam itself, a distinct discipline of 'Islamic economics' emerged

Haider Naqvi, M. A. Mannan and Umer Chapra. It raises the fundamental question of whether an Islamic economy is plan-based or market-based. It also discusses some of the important methodological assumptions of Islamic economics, such as 'Islamic man'.

## *Is an Islamic economy plan-based or market based?*

In an in-depth and comprehensive review of various strands of Islamic economics, Nomani and Rahnema (1994) have analysed all the major tenets of Islamic economics. They argue that the primary sources of *shari'a* – the *Quran* and *hadith* – legitimise the concepts of a free market economy, whereas the secondary sources, and in particular those developed in recent decades, legitimise a planned economy. In fact, Nomani and Rahnema (1994: 55) concede that:

> [A]n economic system built on the strict letter of the [Islamic] law would resemble a perfectly competitive market system. This will be called the 'Islamic market mechanism'. An economic system rigidly built on the equitable spirit of the law would resemble an egalitarian system in which the plan would have to become the coordinating mechanism of the economy. This will be called the 'Islamic plan mechanism'.

only in the twentieth century. For the purpose of this article, therefore, the benchmark for discussion is this modern discipline. According to Dr Ayub Mehar, the term 'Islamic economics' was first used by Shah Wali Ullah, an eighteenth-century leading Islamic philosopher based in India (personal conversation with the author, 2 May 2012).

The authors cite leading jurists and scholars in support of this seemingly self-contradictory and incoherent finding. However, in the final analysis they seem to incline towards a planned economy by stressing the secondary sources. This is evident in their solution, which they call the 'Islamic plan-then-market mechanism' (Nomani and Rahnema 1994: 55). Thus, it is likely that, despite the unambiguously libertarian principles of Islamic economics, the authors have been influenced by modern historical and intellectual developments resulting in socialist and statist philosophies.

Nomani and Rahnema (1994) also believe that the primary aim of an Islamic government is to meet the basic needs of the poor. However, a contrasting 'aim' is found in Islam's traditions and medieval understanding: 'Easing production and distribution of commodities is the most important objective of exchange in the *shari'a*' (Ibn-e Ashur, quoted in Bashar 1997: 40).

Nomani and Rahnema (1994: 65) hold that, once a state has achieved the goal of tending to the poor, it can afford the luxury of adopting a free market: 'According to the plan-then-market coordinating mechanism, during the post-need-fulfilment phase, having established social justice, the Islamic economy can then go back to the letter of the law by adopting the Islamic market allocation, distribution and reward.' Thus they call for a planned transition from the state to the market-based system. However, they seem unaware that once the genie of planning is out of the bottle, it becomes impossible to limit it to any specific time or scope. This genie grows mechanically over time, in the form of state bureaucracy, and by the force of its own inertia tries to envelop everything. Those Islamic economists advocating social coordination in the name of social justice seem unable to understand how bureaucracy permeates the very fabric of human life and perpetuates rent seeking.

M. A. Mannan, a pioneer of Islamic economics, captured the gist of his discipline thus: 'In an Islamic economy, the heart of the problem lies not in the prices offered by the market, but in the existing level of inequality of income' (Mannan 1984: 140). This passage aptly reflects the tension between economic freedom (price) and social justice (inequality). Islamic economics has concerned itself with the causes of poverty rather than the causes of prosperity. It discusses wealth redistribution more enthusiastically than wealth creation, which suggests that modern Islamic economists understand shari'a to sanction a plan-based economy and to focus on reducing income equalities.

Consider, for instance, Syed Nawab Haider Naqvi (2003: 15), another towering figure of the discipline who has argued in favour of forced redistribution of wealth, claiming such a policy Islamic. He writes that:

> for Islamic moral values to become a source of social binding, Muslim societies must be re-organized on the basis of human freedom, social justice and a commitment to help the poor and the needy by restoring to them from the wealth of the rich what is morally and legally theirs as a matter of right.

Naqvi is not alone in conflating moral injunctions of charity with the legal principles. In fact, he led an important official commission set up at the advent of the Islamisation of the economy in Pakistan. To cite another example of this conflation, it is instructive to see how this commission defined the private property from a so-called Islamic perspective. The commission, following in the footsteps of most Islamic economists, developed the argument that in Islam, 'all wealth belongs to Allah' and 'man is only a trustee of whatever he has and not its owner' (Naqvi et al. 1980: 3). This argument has been used consistently to negate the central tenet of private property. However, it should be obvious that as owners we take all the decisions to acquire or dispose of property but we always undertake it under a law – whether secular or divine. We do not ask the lawgivers to complete such transactions on our behalf. The same commission even suggested the introduction of an inheritance tax – of up to 30 per cent – for non-family heirs over and above the explicit Quranic code of distribution of inheritance among legal family heirs. Isn't the suggestion of this tax to include non-family heirs a case of playing God?

## *Can the market be held accountable for distributive justice?*

Mainstream Islamic economists treat distributive justice as a touchstone of economic policy. Like socialists, these economists would hold the market responsible for poverty and inequality. They view private ownership as exploitative. They confound the moral injunctions of the Prophet with canonical law. For example, in expounding his theory of social justice, Ahmad Hassan (1971) relies on Imam Ghazali (d. 1111), a leading Muslim jurist of the medieval era. According to Hassan, Al-Ghazali defined five fundamental human rights, namely, rights to the protection of religion, of life, of reason, of posterity and of property. This list clearly calls for an essentially protective, not a distributive, policy on part of the state. Imam Ghazali advocated the notion of 'negative freedom'. But this point is lost on our friends. Indeed, Hassan (1971: 212) so distorts Al-Ghazali's reasoning as to argue that 'the Quran insists on providing the basic necessities of life to all the members of the Muslim society'. As a matter of record, the Quranic text contains no such injunction. Sadly, some Islamic economists do not even spare the *Quran* in trying to bolster their arguments.

While Hassan may be regarded as an extreme example of an Islamic socialist, writing in the heyday of Communism, the role of justice in economic policy confuses even those scholars who have otherwise established freedom of trade as an 'over-riding factor of the *shari'a*'s price control rulings' (Kamali 1994: 26). Consider this passage by the same author (Kamali 2008: 7; emphasis added):

> Justice is the cardinal duty, indeed the *raison d'être*, of the [Islamic] government not only in its retributive sense of adjudicating grievances but also in the sense of *distributive justice, of establishing equilibrium of benefits and advantages in the community.*

Kamali's distributive justice is a far cry from retributive justice, and a far cry from the essence of Islam's message on economic rewards. How can a system guaranteeing freedom of trade ensure an 'equilibrium of benefits and advantages'? Freedom ought to result in unequal benefits, and as we know, inequality is a permissible, even desired, state in an Islamic economy. The essence of justice is freedom, not equality. This relationship between liberty and justice was best established by Ibn-e Khaldun, the best-known medieval Islamic scholar for founding sociology and for his masterpiece, *Muqadimmah*. He wrote, 'Whoever takes someone's property, or uses him for forced labour, or presses an unjustified claim upon him, it should be known that this is what the Lawgiver had in mind when He forbade injustice'.[3] The Islamic economist Muhammad Abdul Mannan writes: 'Market prices may not enable all the potential consumers and producers to enter into the market' (Mannan 1984: 136). He is right about this, but in fact prices function as means of expression of preference. Like most Islamic economists, Mannan also confuses the concept of freedom with the concept of ability.[4] Freedom is essentially determined by the absence of coercion, particularly coercion from lawful authority, but also coercion from other humans. If a person lacks the ability, or the favourable circumstances, to enter a market, then this is

---

3   Ibn Khaldun (http://sunnahonline.com/ilm/seerah/0033.htm).

4   Amartya Sen (1999) should be given credit for creating the deep confusion between the concepts of freedom and capability. He believes that if a person is poor then he is not free.

not due to coercion. Just as Ibn-e Khaldun elaborated, the spirit of justice is the absence of coercion.

Not all Islamic economists have expressed reservations about the institution of the market. But it is noteworthy that those who favour the market come from non-economic backgrounds. Consider these foundations of the Islamic economy elaborated by S. M. Yusuf, a professor of Arabic: (a) no corner market (that is, no hoarding); (b) no hoarding of gold and silver; (c) no price controls; (d) no restrictions on trade[5]; and (e) the maintenance of the gold standard (Yusuf 1990: 40). Note that Yusuf's understanding of an Islamic economy is 'negative' in character, a spirit much closer to the original, least restrictive attitude towards the market.

## *The moral engineering of the individual: the predicament of Islamic economics*

Muhammad Nejatullah Siddiqi is one of the most important authorities on Islamic economics in the modern age. For him, Islamic economics questions some of the fundamental assumptions of modern economic theory, for instance about human behaviour that is understood as equivalent to self-interest. According to Siddiqi (2001), Islamic economics would be built on the transformation of individual behaviour. Human behaviour has emerged as a favourite topic of discussion among Islamic economists.

---

5   During the course of the research for this chapter, I have been struck by the evidence of free trade even with enemies (except in arms and weapons) during the Prophet's time.

They rightly know that without the transformation of the individual into Islamic man, free of selfishness, the dream of an Islamic economy, living up to its own ideals, will not materialise. In other words, Islamists envisage nothing short of social engineering to purge impure human beings of their illicit desires. For instance, another popular Islamic economist, M. Umer Chapra, recognises the efficiency of the market strategy but believes that human beings need to be reformed (Chapra 1993: 127). However, in this presumptuous approach towards the individual lies a possible predicament for Islamic economists: how to change human nature first? Thus, Islamic economists build the foundations of Islamic economics on the assumption of specific human conduct instead of certain methodologies and principles.

## Conclusion

The foregoing analysis has sought to show that while *shari'a* calls for the establishment of an order of economic freedom based on mutual consent and stringent consumer protection measures, the modern discipline of Islamic economics seems to have drifted in the opposite direction. With few exceptions, mainstream Islamic economics prefers to discuss poverty instead of wealth creation, income differences rather than prices, and the role of the state rather than the role of the market. Notably, Islamic economics is built on the assumption of an imaginary 'Islamic man' who responds to different incentives from those that motivate ordinary human beings. This approach has essentially developed an intellectual framework that provides a spiritual justification of both market-based and plan-based economies without necessarily taking a clear position on principles, methodology and legal framework. However, the general tone of modern Islamic economics remains statist and redistributive. The discipline of Islamic economics that originated in the twentieth century exhibits strong distributive and socialist tendencies in its epistemological assumptions and policy prescriptions. Thus, Islamic economics has shown intellectual leanings towards social justice as a touchstone of economic policy. This has influenced Muslim public opinion and encouraged the largely unelected rulers of Muslim countries to follow predominantly statist, redistributive and even socialist economic policies.

On the other hand, the tradition of Islamic jurisprudence, and in particular its rulings on economic policy, has endorsed a market-friendly, liberal and limited-government philosophy, though subtle and important differences remain between various schools of thought. If the jurists generally stood for economic freedom, why have redistributive tendencies crept into the work of modern Islamic economists?

The classical jurists of Islam are separated from their modern counterparts by the sharp historical wedge that is known as colonialism. The rise of Islamic economics, against the backdrop of a resurgence of the Islamisation of knowledge, is essentially a twentieth-century phenomenon that invites comparison with the gaining of independence on the part of a majority of Muslim countries or their defeat at the hands of Western powers. That has led to the creation of novelties like Islamic socialism or Islamic capitalism, whereas the economic exegesis of the medieval Muslim jurists is free from any such epistemological apologies.

The original spirit of Islamic economic policy as expounded in *shari'a* was protective, non-interventionist, and non-redistributive in character. It looked on market participants and especially traders as benign 'trustees of God on earth', and prescribed legal restrictions on the state discouraging its intervention in markets. The conclusion of this chapter is that Islamic law, as demonstrated in both revealed knowledge and human exegesis, has endorsed a market-friendly, liberal and limited-government philosophy, which we may characterise as libertarian.

Islam was introduced by a Prophet, who led an active life as a merchant for 40 long years and who is reported to have said: 'Welfare and blessedness is composed of ten parts, nine-tenths of which is attained through trade.' This is possible only if the economy is organised on enterprise-centric rather than state-centric lines. The letter of *shari'a* guarantees economic freedom, and its spirit enjoins social justice. The spirit of welfare, which Islam propagates, is based on the degree of choice and freedom that individuals enjoy, and is dependent on the absence of coercion. Welfare does not come from a big state; it comes from prosperous and responsible individuals who imbibe the notion of mutual goodwill and charity towards others.

The *Quran* makes it categorically clear that what an individual receives flows either from his own efforts or from

God's bounty, a favour he does not necessarily deserve. The *Quran* says, 'Man can have nothing but that he strives for' (53: 39). And on many occasions it mentions the Lord's bounty as a favour from Him. For instance, it says, 'Allah may reward them [according to] the best of what they did and increase them from His bounty. And Allah gives provision to whom He wills without account' (24: 38). A *hadith* says that our faith swings like a pendulum between fear and hope; likewise, our sustenance, our economic achievements, oscillate between our effort and our luck. For intellectual convenience, this comes very close to a Misesian understanding of human effort and human design.

Let me finish this essay with a sober reminder from Bastiat, who began his treatise *The Law*, first published in 1850, by treating human life – physical, intellectual and moral – as the sole gift from God, whose preservation, development and perfection is our responsibility (Bastiat 2007: 58):

> God has given to men all that is necessary for them to accomplish their destinies. He has provided a social form as well as a human form. And these social organs of persons are so constituted that they will develop themselves harmoniously in the clean air of liberty. Away, then, with quacks and organizers! Away with their artificial systems! Away with the whims of governmental administrators, their socialized projects, their centralization, their tariffs, their government schools, their state religions, their free credit, their bank monopolies, their regulations, their restrictions, their equalization by

taxation, and their pious moralizations! ... And now that the legislators and do-gooders have so futilely inflicted so many systems upon society, may they finally end where they should have begun: May they reject all systems, and try liberty; for liberty is an acknowledgement of faith in God and His works.

Such is the design of the Mighty One, the all-knowing.

# REFERENCES

Ackroyd, P. (1999) *The Life of Thomas More*. New York: Anchor Books.

Agamben, G. (1998) *Homo Sacer: Sovereign Power and Bare Life*. Redwood City, CA: Stanford University Press.

Ali, A. Y. (1934) *The Meaning of the Glorious Quran*. Islamic Books.

Ambrose (1896) Select works and letters. In *A Select Library of Nicene and Post-Nicene Fathers*, 2nd series, vol. 10. Oxford: Parker.

Ambrose (2001) *De Officiis*, vol. 1 (ed. and trans. I. J. Davidson). Oxford University Press.

Amin, M. (1975) Un acte de foundation de *waqf* par une Chrétienne (Xe siècle h., XVIe s. chr.). *Journal of the Economic and Social History of the Orient* 18(1): 43–52.

Anderson, W. A. (ed.) (1997) *Ovid's Metamorphoses,* Books 1–5. Norman, OK: University of Oklahoma Press.

Angel, M. (1858) *The Law of Sinai, and Its Appointed Times*. London: William Tegg.

Bailey, A. E. and Kent, C. F. (1920) *History of the Hebrew Commonwealth*. New York: Charles Scribner's Sons.

Baker, D. (2009) *Tight Fists or Open Hands? Wealth and Poverty in Old Testament Law*. Grand Rapids, MI: Eerdmans.

Barclay, P. (2011) The evolution of charitable behaviour and the power of reputation. In *Applied Evolutionary Psychology* (ed. C. Roberts), pp. 149–72. Oxford University Press.

Barro, R. and McCleary, R. (2019) *The Wealth of Religions: The Political Economy of Believing and Belonging.* Princeton University Press.

Bashar, M. L. A. (1997) Price control in an Islamic economy. *Journal of King Abdul Aziz University: Islamic Economics* 9: 29–52.

Bastiat, F. (2007) *The Law.* New York: Foundation for Economic Freedom.

Batson, C. D. (2011) *Altruism in Humans.* New York: Oxford University Press.

Bauer, P. (1971) *Dissent on Development: Studies and Debates in Development Economics.* London: Weidenfeld & Nicolson.

Behrens-Abouseif, D. (1994) *Egypt's Adjustment to Ottoman Rule: Institutions, Waqf and Architecture in Cairo.* Leiden: Brill.

Bell, S. G. (1967) Johan Eberlin von Günzburg's 'Wolfaria': the first Protestant utopia. *Church History* 36(2): 122–39.

Berlin, I. (1958) *Two Concepts of Liberty.* Oxford: Clarendon Press.

Berman, E. (2000) Sect, subsidy and sacrifice: an economist's view of ultra-orthodox Jews. *Quarterly Journal of Economics* 115(3): 905–53.

Berman, J. A. (1995) *The Temple: Its Symbolism and Meaning: Then and Now.* New York: Jason Aronson.

Berman, J. A. (2008) *Created Equal: How the Bible Broke with Ancient Political Thought.* Oxford and New York: Oxford University Press.

Blackstone, W. (1765–69) Of property, in general. *Commentaries on the Laws of England*, Book ll, Chapter 1. Oxford: Clarendon Press (http://files.libertyfund.org/files/2140/Blackstone_1387-01_EBk_v6.0.pdf).

Bostaph, S. (2006) Utopia from an economist's perspective. *Thomas More Studies* 1: 196–98.

Brennan, J. (2007) 'Rawls' Paradox'. *Constitutional Political Economy* 18: 287–99.

Burckhardt, J. (1853) *Die Zeit Constantins des Grossen*. Bern: Delphi (1949).

Caetani, L. (1907) *Annali d'Islam*, vol. 2(i). Milan: Ulrico Hoepli.

Cahen, C. (1961) Réflexions sur le *Waqf* ancient. *Studia Islamica* 14: 37–56.

Chapra, M. U. (1993) *Islam and Economic Development*. Islamabad: International Institute of Islamic Thought.

Cicero, Marcus Tullius (1913) *De Officiis* (trans. W. Miller). London: Heinemann.

Cicero, Marcus Tullius (2006) *Speech on Behalf of Publius Sestius* (ed. and trans. R. Kaster). Oxford University Press.

Coleman, J. (1985) Dominium in thirteenth and fourteenth-century political thought and its seventeenth-century heirs: John of Paris and John Locke. *Political Studies* 33(1): 73–100.

Comte, A. (1865 [2009]) *A General View of Positivism*. Cambridge University Press.

Davis, J. C. (1981) *Utopia and the Ideal Society: A Study of English Utopian Writing 1516–1700*. Cambridge University Press.

Davis, R. (trans.) (2000) *The Book of Pontiffs* (*Liber Pontificalis*): *The Ancient Biographies of First Ninety Roman Bishops to AD 715*. Liverpool University Press.

Dawood, N. J. (trans.) (1999) *The Koran*. London: Penguin.

de Vaux, R. (1961) *Ancient Israel: Its Life and Institutions*. London: Darton, Longman and Todd.

Dewey, J. (1926) The historic background of corporate legal personality. *Yale Law Journal* 35(6): 655–73.

Dost, S. (2009) *The Idea of Free Market in Early Islam* (https://www.yumpu.com/en/document/view/42263879/the

-idea-of-free-market-in-early-islam-atlas-economic-res
earch-/7).

Durkheim, E. (1995) *The Elementary Forms of Religious Life.*
(trans. K. E. Fields). New York, NY: The Free Press.

Eidelberg, P. (2005) The Jewish roots of the American Constitution. *Arutz Sheva*, 30 November (http://www.israelnational
news.com/Articles/Article.aspx/5817).

Elon, M. (1975) Taxation. In *The Principles of Jewish Law* (ed. M.
Elon). Jerusalem: Keter.

Fanfani, A. (1934) *Catholicism and Protestantism in the Historical Formation of Capitalism.* Societa Editrice Vita e Pennsiero.

Fehr, E. and Gächter, S. (2000) Fairness and retaliation: the economics of reciprocity. *Journal of Economic Perspectives* 14(3):
159–81.

Frank, R. (1987) If *homo economicus* could choose his own utility function, would he want one with a conscience? *American
Economic Review* 77(4): 593–604.

Frayer, L. (2016) As Israel's ultra-orthodox enter the workforce,
high-tech beckons. *Parallels*, 12 November (http://www.npr
.org/sections/parallels/2016/11/12/501620376/as-israels-ultra
-orthodox-enter-the-workforce-high-tech-beckons).

Friedman, D. (1973 [1978]) *The Machinery of Freedom.* New Ro-
chelle, NY: Arlington House.

Friedman, M. (1991) Say 'no' to intolerance. *Liberty* 4(6): 17–20.

Gaudiosi, M. (1988) The influence of the Islamic law of *waqf* on
the development of the trust in England: the case of Merton
College. *University of Pennsylvania Law Review* 136(4): 1231–61.

Gera, D. L. (1993) *Xenophon's* Cyropaedia*: Style, Genre, and Literary Technique.* Oxford: Clarendon Press.

Giardina, A. (2007) The transition to late antiquity. In *The Cambridge Economic History of the Greco-Roman World* (ed. W. Scheidel et al.). Cambridge University Press.

Gil, M. (1984) Dhimmi donations and foundations for Jerusalem (638–1099). *Journal of the Economic and Social History of the Orient* 27(4): 156–74.

Gil, M. (1998) The earliest *waqf* foundations. *Journal of Near Eastern Studies* 57(2): 125–40.

Gillespie, M. A. (2008) *The Theological Origins of Modernity.* University of Chicago Press.

Goodman, H. (2011) *The Anatomy of Israel's Survival.* New York: Public Affairs.

Gordis, D. (2011) The shape and meaning of biblical history. *Azure* 45 (http://azure.org.il/include/print.php?id=579).

Gordon, B. (1989) *The Economic Problem in Biblical and Patristic Thought.* Leiden: Brill.

Grace, D. (1989) Utopia: a dialectical interpretation. *Moreana* 26(100): 274–302.

Gregg, S. (2013a) What is social justice? Library of Law and Liberty (http://www.libertylawsite.org/liberty-forum/what-is-social-justice/).

Gregg, S. (2013b) *Tea Party Catholic: The Catholic Case for Limited Government, a Free Economy and Human Flourishing.* New York: Crossroad Publishing Company.

Gregory, P. R. and Stuart, R. C. (2004) *Comparative Economic Systems in the Twenty-First Century.* Boston, MA: Houghton-Mifflin Company.

Grey, A. (1933) *The Development of Economic Doctrine.* London: Longmans, Green and Co.

Guignebert, C. (1901) *Tertullien. Étude sur ses sentiments a l'égard de l'empire et de la société civile.* Paris: Ernest Leroux.

Gwartney, J., Lawson, R., Hall, J. and Murphy, R. (2018) *Economic Freedom of the World: 2018 Annual Report.* Fraser Institute.

Habig, M. A. (ed.) (1983) *Francis of Assisi: Writings and Early Biographies.* Chicago, IL: Franciscan Herald Press.

Hariyanto, S. (1995) *Nasreddin, The Wise Man.* Yogyakarta: Penerbit Kanisus.

Hassan, A. (1971) Social justice in Islam. *Islamic Studies* 10(3): 209–19.

Hayek, F. A. (1960) *The Constitution of Liberty.* University of Chicago Press.

Hayek, F. A. (1973) *Rules and Order.* Law, Legislation and Liberty, 1. London: Routledge and Kegan Paul.

Hayek, F. A. (1976) *The Mirage of Social Justice.* Law, Legislation and Liberty, 2. London: Routledge and Kegan Paul.

Hazony, Y. (2005) Judaism and the modern state. *Azure* 21: 33–52.

Hejcl, J. (1907) *Das alttestamentliche Zinsverbot im Lichte der ethnologischen Jurisprudenz sowie des altorientalischen Zinswesens.* Freiburg: Herder.

Hennigan, P. (2004) *The Birth of a Legal Institution: The Formation of the Waqf in Third-Century A. H. Hanafi.* Legal Discourse. Leiden: Brill.

Henrich, J. (2020) *The Weirdest People in the World. How the West Became Psychologically Peculiar and Particularly Prosperous.* London: Allen Lane.

Hodgson, G. M. (2013) *From Pleasure Machines to Moral Communities: An Evolutionary Economics without Homo Economicus.* University of Chicago Press.

Hoexter, M. (1998) Waqf studies in the twentieth century: the state of the art. *Journal of the Economic and Social History of the Orient* 41(4): 474–95.

Hoppe, H. H. (1989) *A Theory of Socialism and Capitalism.* Boston, Dordrecht and London: Kluwer Academic Publishers.

Hosseini, H. S. (2003) Contributions of medieval Muslim scholars to the history of economics and their impact: a refutation of the Schumpeterian Great Gap. In *A Companion to the History of Economic Thought* (ed. W. Samuels, J. Biddle and J. Davis). Malden, MA: Blackwell.

Iannaccone, L. R. (1998) Introduction to the economics of religion. *Journal of Economic Literature* 36(3): 1465–95.

Ibn Hanbal, A. (2012) *Musnad* (3 vols). Riyadh: Dar-us-Salam Publications.

Ibn Sa'd, M. (1995) *The Women of Madina: Tabaqat*, vol. VIII (trans. A. Bewley). London: Ta-Ha Publishers.

Ibn Sa'd, M. (1997) *The Men of Madina*, vol. 1. London: Ta-Ha Publishers.

Ibn Sa'd, M. (2012) *Kitab At-Tabaqat Al-Kabir*, vol. VI: *The Scholars of Kufa*. London: Ta-Ha Publishers.

Ibn S'ad, M. (2013) *Kitab At-Tabaqat Al-Kabir*, vol. III: *The Companions of Badr*. London: Ta-Ha Publishers.

Iyer, S. (2016) The new economics of religion. *Journal of Economic Literature* 54(2): 395–441.

Jackson, M. (2000) Imagined republics: Machiavelli, utopia, and 'Utopia'. *Journal of Value Inquiry* 34(4): 427–37.

John Chrysostomos (1888) Homilies on the Gospel of Saint Matthew. In *A Select Library of Nicene and Post-Nicene Fathers*, vol. X (ed. P. Schaff). Edinburgh: T. & T. Clark.

John Paul II (2000). *Moto proprio* (31 October) on 'Proclaiming St. Thomas More a patron of statesmen and politicians'. Vatican: Libreria Editrice Vaticana (http://w2.vatican.va/content/john -paul-ii/en/motu_proprio/documents/hf_jp-ii_motu-proprio _20001031_thomas-more.html).

Julian the Apostate (1923) *The Works of the Emperor Julian*, vol. 3 (trans. W. C. Wright). London. William Heinemann.

Jursa, M. (2015) Market performance and market integration in Babylonia in the 'long sixth century' BC. In *A History of Market Performance: From Ancient Babylonia to the Modern World* (ed. R. van der Spek, J. van Sanden and Bas van Leeuwen). Abingdon: Routledge.

Kamali, M. H. (1994) *Tas'ir* (price control) in Islamic Law. *American Journal of Islamic Social Sciences* 11(1): 25–37.

Kamali, M. H. (2008) *Maqasid Al-Shari'a Made Simple.* Occasional Paper 13. London and Washington, DC: International Institute of Advanced Islamic Studies.

Kandori, M. (1992) Social norms and community enforcement. *Review of Economic Studies* 59: 63–80.

Kanter, R. M. (1972) *Commitment and Community: Communes and Utopias in Sociological Perspective.* Cambridge, MA: Harvard University Press.

Kautsky, K. (1888 [1959]) *Thomas More and His Utopia.* New York: Russell & Russell.

Kessler, S. (2002) Religious freedom in Thomas More's *Utopia. Review of Politics* 64(2): 207–29.

Klemon, J. (2012) The state of Haredi education in the state of Israel. Foreign Policy Association (http://foreignpolicyblogs .com/2012/02/05/state-haredi-education-state-israel/).

Knight, F. (1939) Ethics and economic reform. III. Christianity. *Economica* (New Series) 6(24): 398–422.

Knight, F. and Merriam, T. (1947) *The Economic Order and Religion.* London: Kegan Paul.

Krautheimer, R. (1983) *Three Christian Capitals: Topography and Politics.* Berkeley and Los Angeles, CA: University of California Press.

Kuran, T. (2001) The provision of public goods under Islamic law: origins, impact, and limitations of the *waqf* system. *Law and Society Review* 35(4): 841–98.

Kuran, T. (2005) The absence of the corporation in Islamic law: origins and persistence. *American Journal of Comparative Law* 53(4): 785–834.

Kuran, T. (2010) *The Long Divergence: How Islamic Law Held Back the Middle East.* Princeton University Press.

Kurun, I. (2016) *The Theological Origins of Liberalism.* Lanham, MD: Lexington Books.

Laffer, A. (2004) *The Laffer Curve: Past, Present, and Future.* Washington, DC: Heritage Foundation.

Lambert, M. (1998) *Franciscan Poverty: The Doctrine of Absolute Poverty of Christ and the Apostles in the Franciscan Order, 1210–1323.* St. Bonaventure, NY: Franciscan Institute.

Laum, B. (1914) *Stiftungen in der griechischen und römischen Antike*, vol. 2. Leipzig: Teubner.

Leiter, Y. (2008) The Hebraic roots of John Locke's doctrine of charity. *Jerusalem Political Studies Review* 20 (3–4).

Lev, Y. (2005) *Charity, Endowments, and Charitable Institutions in Medieval Islam.* Gainesville, FL: University Press of Florida.

Lewis, C. and Short, C. (1879) *A Latin Dictionary Founded on Andrews' Edition of Freund's Latin Dictionary.* Oxford: Clarendon Press.

Lifshitz, Y. Y. (2004) Foundations of a Jewish economic theory. *Azure* 18: 34–66.

Lowenberg, F. M. (2001) *From Charity to Social Justice.* Brunswick, NJ: Transaction Books.

Maccoby, H. (1996) *A Pariah People: The Anthropology of Antisemitism.* London: Constable.

Maimon, D. and Rosner, S. (2013) The Haredi challenge. The Jewish People Policy Institute, 21 February (http://jppi.org.il/new/en/article/english-the-haredi-challenge/#.WO_AWGe1vcs).

Maitland, F. W. (1894) 'The origin of uses'. *Harvard Law Review* 8(3): 127–37.

Mannan, M. A. (1984) *The Frontiers of Islamic Economics.* Delhi: Idarah-e Adabiyat-e Delli.

Marius, R. (1984) *Thomas More: A Biography.* Cambridge, MA: Harvard University Press.

Maslow, A. (1943) A theory of human motivation. *Psychological Review* 50(4): 370–96.

Maslow, A. (1969) The farther reaches of human nature. *Journal of Transpersonal Psychology* 1(1): 1–9.

Mason, J. D. (1987) Biblical teaching and assisting the poor. *Transformation: An International Journal of Holistic Mission Studies* 4(1): 1–14.

Mason, J. D. (1992) Centralization and decentralization in social arrangements. *Journal of the Association of Christian Economists* 13: 39–52.

Michaelis, J. (1814) *Commentaries on the Laws of Moses* (trans. from *Mosaisches Recht* of 1785 by A. Smith), vol. 1. London.

Mill, J. S. (1859) *On Liberty.* London: John W. Parker and Son.

Mill, J. S. (1861 [1991]) Considerations on representative government. In *On Liberty and Other Essays.* Oxford and New York: Oxford University Press.

Mises, L. von (1951) *Socialism: An Economic and Sociological Analysis.* London: Jonathan Cape.

More, T. (1516) *Utopia* (https://www.gutenberg.org/files/2130/2130-h/2130-h.htm). (Page numbers refer to https://quikscan.org/Utopia.pdf.)

Naqvi, S. N. H. (2003) *Perspectives on Morality and Human Well-Being: A Contribution to Islamic Economics.* Leicester: The Islamic Foundation.

Naqvi, S. N. H., Beg, H. U., Ahmed, R. and Nazeer, M. M. (1980) *An Agenda of Islamic Economic Reform: The Report of the Committee on Islamization, appointed by the Finance Minister, Government of Pakistan.* Islamabad: Pakistan Institute of Development Economics.

Nell-Breuning, O. von, S.J. (1932) *Die soziale Enzyklika. Erläuterungen zum Weltrundschreiben Papst Pius XI. über die gesellschaftliche Ordnung.* Köln: Katholische Tat-Verlag.

Nelson, E. (2011) *The Hebrew Commonwealth.* Cambridge, MA, and London: Harvard University Press.

Nelson, E. (2019) *The Theology of Liberalism.* Cambridge, MA: Belknap Press,

Neufeld, E. (1955) The prohibitions against loans at interest in ancient Hebrew laws. *Hebrew Union College Annual* 26: 355–412.

Neusner, J. (1990) *The Economics of the Mishna.* Chicago University Press.

Nobes, C. (2001) Were Islamic records precursors to accounting books based on the Italian method? A comment. *Accounting Historians Journal* 28(2): 207–14.

Noell, E. (2014) Theonomy and economic institutions. In *The Oxford Handbook of Christianity and Economics* (ed. P. Oslington). Oxford University Press.

Nomani, F. and Rahnema, A. (1994) *Islamic Economic Systems.* London: Zed Books.

North, D. (1990). *Institutions, Institutional Change and Economic Performance.* Cambridge University Press.

Nozick, R. (1974) *Anarchy, State and Utopia.* New York: Basic Books.

Oden, R. A. (1984) Taxation in biblical Israel. *Journal of Religious Ethics* 12(2): 162–81.

Olson, M. (1982) *The Rise and Decline of Nations: Economic Growth, Stagflation, and Social Rigidities.* New Haven, CT: Yale University Press.

Oran, A. (2010) An Islamic socio-economic public interest theory of market regulation. *Review of Islamic Economics* 14(1): 125–46.

Ostrom, E. (1998) A behavioral approach to the rational choice theory of collective action. *American Political Science Review* 92(1): 1–22.

Oz-Salzberger, F. (2002) The Jewish roots of Western freedom. *Azure* 13: 88–132.

Oz-Salzberger, F. (2006) The political thought of John Locke and the significance of political Hebraism. *Hebraic Political Studies* 1(5): 568–92.

Pahlitzsch, J. (2009) Christian pious foundations as an element between Late Antiquity and Islam. In *Charity and Giving in*

*Monotheistic Religions* (ed. M. Frenkel and Y. Lev). Berlin: de Gruyter.

Paley, M. R. (2006) *Orthodox Judaism, Liberalism, and Libertarianism*. Baltimore, MD: Publish America.

Parrill, S. and Robison, W. B. (2013) *The Tudors on Film and Television*. Jefferson, NC: McFarland.

Paris, D. (1998). An economic look at the Old Testament. In *Ancient and Medieval Economic Ideas and Concepts of Social Justice* (ed. S. Todd Lowry and B. Gordon). Leiden: Brill.

Perikhanian, A. (1983) Iranian society and law. In *The Cambridge History of Iran* (ed. E. Yarshater), vol. 3(2). Cambridge University Press.

Piketty, T. (2013) *Le capital au XXIe siècle*. Paris: Editions du Seuil.

Plutarch (1914) *The Parallel Lives by Plutarch*, vol. 1. London: Loeb Classical Library (https://penelope.uchicago.edu/Thayer/e/roman/texts/plutarch/lives/home.html).

Ratzinger, G. (1868) *Geschichte der kirchlichen Armenpflege*. Freiburg: Herdersche Verlagshandlung.

Rawls, J. (1971) *A Theory of Justice*. Cambridge, MA: Harvard University Press.

Rhonheimer, M. (2011) *The Perspective of Morality: Philosophical Foundations of Thomistic Virtue Ethics*. Washington, DC: Catholic University of America Press.

Rhonheimer, M. (2013) John XXIII's *Pacem in terris* – The First Human Rights Encyclical. In *Il concetto di pace: attualità della Pacem in Terris nel 50° anniversario (1963–2013)* (ed. V. V. Alberti). Città del Vaticano: Libreria Editrice Vaticana (published by the Pontifical Council of Justice and Peace).

Rivlin, R. (2015) Address to the 15th Annual Herzliya Conference, 7 June (https://docslib.org/doc/6961923/president-reuven-riv lin-address-to-the-15th-annual-herzliya-conference-israeli -hope-towards-a-new-israeli-order-7-june-2015-20-sivan -5775).

Rodinson, M. (1966) *Islam et Capitalisme*. Paris: Éditions du Seuil.

Rodinson, M. (1973) Préface. In *El 'señor del zoco' en España: edades media y moderna* (ed. P. Chalmeta). Madrid: Instituto Hispano-Arabe de Cultura.

Röpke, W. (1944) *Civitas humana. Grundfragen der Gesellschaftsund Wirtschaftsreform*. Erlenbach-Zürich: Eugen Rentsch Verlag.

Rosmini, A. (1994) *Society and Its Purpose*. Durham: Rosmini House. (Originally published as *La società e il suo fine*, Milan, 1837.)

Rosmini, A. (2007) *The Constitution Under Social Justice* (trans. A. Mingardi). Lanham, MD: Rowman and Littlefield, Lexington Books. (Originally published as *La Costituzione secondo la giustizia sociale con un'appendice sull'unità d'Italia*, Naples, 1848.)

Rothbard, M. N. (1973) *For a New Liberty: The Libertarian Manifesto* (revised edition). New York and London: Collier.

Rothbard, M. (2006) *Economic Thought Before Adam Smith: An Austrian Perspective on the History of Economic Thought*, vol. I. Auburn, AL: Ludwig von Mises Institute.

Sarna, N. (1991) *Exodus: The JPS Commentary. Philadelphia*. Philadelphia, PA: The Jewish Publication Society.

Schumpeter, J. (1954) *History of Economic Analysis*. London: Allen & Unwin.

Schwartz, P. (1989) Imagining socialism: Karl Kautsky and Thomas More. *International Journal of Comparative Sociology* 30(1): 44–56.

Sedláček, T. (2011) *Economics of Good and Evil: The Quest for Economic Meaning from Gilgamesh to Wall Street.* Oxford University Press.

Sen, A. (1999) *Development as Freedom.* Oxford University Press.

Senor, D. and Singer, S. (2009) *Start-Up Nation: The Story of Israel's Economic Miracle.* New York: Twelve.

Siddiqi, M. N. (2001) *Economics: An Islamic Approach.* Islamabad: Institute of Policy Studies and The Islamic Foundation.

Siedentop, L. (2014) *Inventing the Individual: The Origins of Western Liberalism.* London: Allen Lane.

Smith, A. (1776 [1937]) *An Inquiry into the Nature and Causes of the Wealth of Nations.* New York: Modern Library.

Smith, W. R. (1889) *The Religion of the Semites.* London: Adam & Charles Black.

Sozomen (1855) *The Eccesiastical History of Sozomen, Comprising a History of the Church from A.D. 324 to A.D. 440* (trans. E. Walford). London: Bohn.

Spengler, J. (1980) *Origins of Economic Thought and Justice.* Carbondale, IL: Southern Illinois University Press.

Sprenger, A. (1856a) Über das Traditionswesen bei den Arabern. *Zeitschrift der deutschen morgenländischen Gesellschaft* 10: 1–17.

Sprenger, A. (1856b) Notes on Alfred von Kremer's edition of Waqidy's campaigns. *Journal of the Asiatic Society of Bengal* 25: 53–74, 199–220.

Sprenger, A. (1856c) On the origin and progress of writing down historical facts among the Musulmans. *Journal of the Asiatic Society of Bengal* 25: 303–29, 375–81.

Syed, M., Akhtar, S. and Usmani, B. (eds) (2011) *A Concise History of Islam*. New Delhi: Vij Books.

Tamari, M. (1987) *With All Your Possessions: Jewish Ethics and Economic Life*. New York and London: The Free Press.

Taparelli d'Azeglio, L. (1883) *Saggio teoretico di dritto naturale appoggiato sul fatto*, vol. 1 (2nd edn). Prato: Tipografia Giachetti.

Tawney, R. H. (1926) *Religion and the Rise of Capitalism*. London: John Murray.

Tebble, A. J. (2009) Hayek on social justice: a critique. *Critical Review of International Social and Political Philosophy* 12(4): 581–604.

Tertullian (1931) *Apology* (trans. T. R. Glover). London. Heinemann.

Tomasi, J. (2012) *Free Market Fairness*. Princeton University Press.

Uhlhorn, J. G. W. (1883) *Christian Charity in the Ancient Church* (trans. S. Taylor). Edinburgh: T. & T. Clark.

Usmani, R. (2010) *Islami Maeeshat Ki Khasoosiaat Aur San'ati Ta'aluqat*. Karachi: Idara Al Ma'arif.

van Berchem, D. (1939) *La distribution de blé et d'argent à la plèbe de l'empire*. Geneva: Georg et Cie.

van der Spek, R. and Mandemakers, K. (2003) Sense and non-sense in the statistical approach of Babylonian prices. *Bibliotheca Orientalis* 60(5–6): 521–37.

Veblen, T. (1912) *The Theory of the Leisure Class: An Economic Study of Institutions*. London: Macmillan.

Viner, J. (1978) *Religious Thought and Economic Society* (ed. J. Melitz and D. Winch). Durham, NC: Duke University Press.

Voigt, S. and Engerer, H. (2002) Institutions and transformation – possible policy implications of the new institutional economics. In *Frontiers in Economics* (ed. K. Zimmerman), pp. 127–184. Berlin: Springer.

Wayland, F. (1837) *The Elements of Political Economy*. New York: Leavitt, Lord.

Weber, M. (1905 [1930]) *The Protestant Ethic and the Spirit of Capitalism*. First English translation. New York, NY: Scribner.

Weber, M. (1952) *Ancient Judaism* (trans. and ed. H. Gerth and D. Martindale from *Das antike Judentum*, 1921). New York: Free Press.

Westbrook, R. (1985) The price factor in the redemption of land. *Revue internationale des droits de l'antiquité* 32: 97–127.

Wines, E. (1853) *Commentaries on the Laws of the Ancient Hebrews*. Philadelphia, PA: Presbyterian Board of Publication.

Wood, J. (1999) Sir Thomas More: a man for one season. In *The Broken Estate: Essays on Literature and Belief* (ed. J. Wood), pp. 3–15. New York: Random House.

Wulff, H. E. (1968) The Qanats of Iran. *Scientific American* 218(4): 94–105.

Yusuf, S.M. (1990) *Economic Justice in Islam*. Islamabad: Da'wah Academy.

Zion, N. (2012) *The Ethics of Economics: Israeli–Haredim and Israeli Arabs – The Duty to Work and the Duty to Provide Work*. Jerusalem: Shalom Hartman Institute.

## ABOUT THE IEA

The Institute is a research and educational charity (No. CC 235 351), limited by guarantee. Its mission is to improve understanding of the fundamental institutions of a free society by analysing and expounding the role of markets in solving economic and social problems.

The IEA achieves its mission by:

- a high-quality publishing programme
- conferences, seminars, lectures and other events
- outreach to school and college students
- brokering media introductions and appearances

The IEA, which was established in 1955 by the late Sir Antony Fisher, is an educational charity, not a political organisation. It is independent of any political party or group and does not carry on activities intended to affect support for any political party or candidate in any election or referendum, or at any other time. It is financed by sales of publications, conference fees and voluntary donations.

In addition to its main series of publications, the IEA also publishes (jointly with the University of Buckingham), *Economic Affairs*.

The IEA is aided in its work by a distinguished international Academic Advisory Council and an eminent panel of Honorary Fellows. Together with other academics, they review prospective IEA publications, their comments being passed on anonymously to authors. All IEA papers are therefore subject to the same rigorous independent refereeing process as used by leading academic journals.

IEA publications enjoy widespread classroom use and course adoptions in schools and universities. They are also sold throughout the world and often translated/reprinted.

Since 1974 the IEA has helped to create a worldwide network of 100 similar institutions in over 70 countries. They are all independent but share the IEA's mission.

Views expressed in the IEA's publications are those of the authors, not those of the Institute (which has no corporate view), its Managing Trustees, Academic Advisory Council members or senior staff.

Members of the Institute's Academic Advisory Council, Honorary Fellows, Trustees and Staff are listed on the following page.

The Institute gratefully acknowledges financial support for its publications programme and other work from a generous benefaction by the late Professor Ronald Coase.

*Other books recently published by the IEA include:*

*Financial Stability without Central Banks*
George Selgin, Kevin Dowd and Mathieu Bédard
ISBN 978-0-255-36752-3; £10.00

*Against the Grain: Insights from an Economic Contrarian*
Paul Ormerod
ISBN 978-0-255-36755-4; £15.00

*Ayn Rand: An Introduction*
Eamonn Butler
ISBN 978-0-255-36764-6; £12.50

*Capitalism: An Introduction*
Eamonn Butler
ISBN 978-0-255-36758-5; £12.50

*Opting Out: Conscience and Cooperation in a Pluralistic Society*
David S. Oderberg
ISBN 978-0-255-36761-5; £12.50

*Getting the Measure of Money: A Critical Assessment of UK Monetary Indicators*
Anthony J. Evans
ISBN 978-0-255-36767-7; £12.50

*Socialism: The Failed Idea That Never Dies*
Kristian Niemietz
ISBN 978-0-255-36770-7; £17.50

*Top Dogs and Fat Cats: The Debate on High Pay*
Edited by J. R. Shackleton
ISBN 978-0-255-36773-8; £15.00

*School Choice around the World … And the Lessons We Can Learn*
Edited by Pauline Dixon and Steve Humble
ISBN 978-0-255-36779-0; £15.00

*School of Thought: 101 Great Liberal Thinkers*
Eamonn Butler
ISBN 978-0-255-36776-9; £12.50

*Raising the Roof: How to Solve the United Kingdom's Housing Crisis*
Edited by Jacob Rees-Mogg and Radomir Tylecote
ISBN 978-0-255-36782-0; £12.50

*How Many Light Bulbs Does It Take to Change the World?*
Matt Ridley and Stephen Davies
ISBN 978-0-255-36785-1; £10.00

*The Henry Fords of Healthcare ... Lessons the West Can Learn from the East*
Nima Sanandaji
ISBN 978-0-255-36788-2; £10.00

*An Introduction to Entrepreneurship*
Eamonn Butler
ISBN 978-0-255-36794-3; £12.50

*An Introduction to Democracy*
Eamonn Butler
ISBN 978-0-255-36797-4; £12.50

*Having Your Say: Threats to Free Speech in the 21st Century*
Edited by J. R. Shackleton
ISBN 978-0-255-36800-1; £17.50

*The Sharing Economy: Its Pitfalls and Promises*
Michael C. Munger
ISBN 978-0-255-36791-2; £12.50

*An Introduction to Trade and Globalisation*
Eamonn Butler
ISBN 978-0-255-36803-2; £12.50

*Why Free Speech Matters*
Jamie Whyte
ISBN 978-0-255-36806-3; £10.00

*The People Paradox: Does the World Have Too Many or Too Few People?*
Steven E. Landsburg and Stephen Davies
ISBN 978-0-255-36809-4; £10.00

*An Introduction to Economic Inequality*
Eamonn Butler
ISBN 978-0-255-36815-5; £10.00

*Carbon Conundrum: How to Save Climate Change Policy from Government Failure*
Philip Booth and Carlo Stagnaro
ISBN 978-0-255-36812-4; £12.50

*Scaling the Heights: Thought Leadership, Liberal Values and the History of The Mont Pelerin Society*
Eamonn Butler
ISBN 978-0-255-36818-6; £10.00?

## Other IEA publications

Comprehensive information on other publications and the wider work of the IEA can be found at www.iea.org.uk. To order any publication please see below.

## Personal customers

Orders from personal customers should be directed to the IEA:

IEA
2 Lord North Street
FREEPOST LON10168
London SW1P 3YZ
Tel: 020 7799 8911, Fax: 020 7799 2137
Email: sales@iea.org.uk

## Trade customers

All orders from the book trade should be directed to the IEA's distributor:

Ingram Publisher Services UK
1 Deltic Avenue
Rooksley
Milton Keynes MK13 8LD
Tel: 01752 202301, Fax: 01752 202333
Email: ipsuk.orders@ingramcontent.com

## IEA subscriptions

The IEA also offers a subscription service to its publications. For a single annual payment (currently £42.00 in the UK), subscribers receive every monograph the IEA publishes. For more information please contact:

Subscriptions
IEA
2 Lord North Street
FREEPOST LON10168
London SW1P 3YZ
Tel: 020 7799 8911, Fax: 020 7799 2137
Email: accounts@iea.org.uk